Ballyhoo

Mary C. Henderson

The American
Theater Seen
in Posters,
Photographs,
Magazines,
Caricatures,
and Programs

TO MY THREE FINEST CREATIONS,
JIM, DOUG, AND STUART HENDERSON

LIBRARY OF CONGRESS CATALOGING-IN-PUBLICATION DATA

Henderson, Mary C., 1928–   Broadway ballyhoo: the American theater in posters,
photographs, magazines, caricatures, and programs / Mary C. Henderson.
p.   cm.   Bibliography: p. 178   Includes index.   ISBN 0–8109–1889–7
1. Theater—United States—History—Pictorial works.   2. Theatrical posters, American.
3. Arts publicity—United States—History—Pictorial works.   I. Title.
PN2226.H46   1989   792'.0973—dc19   89–89

Project Director: Margaret L. Kaplan
Editor: Ellyn Childs Allison
Designer: Bob McKee
Photo Editor: John K. Crowley

Contents

Preface and Acknowledgments

Today in America, there exists a small industry set up to promote a show from start to finish. Although it began to emerge importantly in the late years of the nineteenth century, when theater as a serious art took a decided turn toward big business, some form of hoopla has always accompanied the launching of a theatrical production. Ringing bells, flying flags, posting notices on every available wall, sending out town criers, dispatching the actors themselves to spread the word, staging a parade, placing notices in newspapers—all these time-tested devices have been used to get the public's attention, and all have been effective, each in its own day and in its own way.

More than a hundred years ago, paunchy men in dark suits took the place of theater managers in dashing and eccentric attire, and they invented show business. Advertising the show, a major preoccupation with this new breed of producers, brought forth an avalanche of printed matter. Posters became bigger and showier, always eye-catching, sometimes even works of art, and they supplanted the early black-and-white printed broadsides, which had given the essential facts along with a few blaring adjectives (SENSATIONAL! TREMENDOUS! GORGEOUS!). Programs were now packed with colorful product advertisements and presented readable features. Newspapers and weekly and monthly magazines were fed stories about the performers and the show—the more provocative the better. Many newspapers and periodicals set up theater departments, and their editors sent out sketch artists to capture the likenesses of the stars. Later, when the technology was in place, not an issue went by that did not contain photographs of the big stars and stage celebrities. Meanwhile, the caricaturist wielded his waggish pen to keep things in balance, pricking the large theatrical egos and cutting the stars down to human scale. Soon, slick magazines sprang up to cover the world of make-believe, loaded with illustrations and photographs, reviews of shows, and all sorts of sweetmeats for the adoring theatrical public. Their lifeblood was the instantaneous photograph, which began its long evolution about mid-century, very nearly coinciding with the drift toward big-time show business and giving new meaning to the star system in America and abroad in the nineteenth century. (When Thomas Edison coaxed the photograph to appear to move, the glory days of theatrical show business began to be numbered.)

Programs, posters, newspaper clippings, magazines, photographs—all this theatrical paper was meant to be ephemeral, and much of it was, in fact, destined to accompany the next day's garbage. But because it had to do with the theater, because aficionados decline to dispose of anything to do with their obsessive interests, because it was colorful and readable and great fun, because a few people decided that it was also history and, once in a while, art, much of what should have disappeared has miraculously survived and migrated to libraries, historical societies, and museums. Today, historical legitimacy has elevated it to the status of "documentation," not merely of theatrical performance but of society. That little cigarette card bearing the likeness of the sumptuous Lillian Russell now unlocks truths about late nineteenth-century society, economics, habits, and tastes. As a tiny piece of a large picture, it now helps us to establish and verify history itself, a heavy burden for such a once-insignificant thing.

The theater has always benefited by advances in advertising technology, and producers continue to use whatever devices are available to sell their wares as supplements to their traditional campaigns in print. Radio spot announcements have been commonplace for many years, and the success of television advertising for the theater has spurred the creation of live ads for shows, despite their great cost. With the advent of home audio and video tape recorders, can we anticipate an added dimension to the preserved records of the show, as collectors wheel up to libraries and museums with their caches of cassettes to deposit with the already over-burdened librarians and curators? Should these records be preserved? Can they be preserved? And where is the money coming from to do it? When this day arrives, librarians and curators will no doubt deal sensibly with the new problems as they have in the past, but the prospect does not brighten their lives.

Although theatrical performance is doomed to become a memory after the final curtain, the trail of mementos has created an afterlife for the theater in America. This book aspires to examine these ephemeral reflections in print, not merely as documentation but as part of the evolution of the living theater during the last hundred or so years, and to show how they affected the course of theater in America—and how in turn they were affected by the very institution they were promoting.

My own interest in these paper recollections of theater comes naturally. As curator of the Theatre Collection of the Museum of the City of New York, for many years I was literally surrounded by tens of thousands of files on theatrical productions and personalities, each containing anything from a crumbling clipping to a full complement of playbills, souvenir programs, photographs, newspaper and magazine articles, and anything else that had happened to migrate into the envelopes. The information they yielded was often fascinating and tantalizing. It helped to create fuller and richer exhibitions by providing bits and pieces of a giant never-to-be completed jigsaw puzzle. Fitting the pieces together becomes an exhilarating experience and sharpens the collecting abilities of all who work with theatrical-paper records.

I pay tribute to all collectors of theatrical ephemera, both private and public. It is to them that I turned in assembling this book. They remained remarkably patient with me while I was searching for that special image I insisted was still in existence (and usually was not). I mention first my colleagues, both past and current, at the Museum of the City of New York: Wendy Warnken, Mary Ann Smith, Bob Taylor, Diane Cypkin, Dolly Hecht, Maxwell Silverman, Stuart Soloway, Camille Dee, David Diamond, and Jennifer Bright, for their valued help and support. My home away from home for many years has been the Theatre Collection of the New York Public Library at Lincoln Center, where I enlisted the aid of the curator, Dorothy Swerdlove, and the able staff, consisting of Donald Fowle, Richard Lynch, David Bartholomew, Olive Wong, Edward Sager, Christine Karatnytsky, Don Madison, Daniel Patri, Heidi Stock, Brian O'Connell, Jack Best, Stephen Vallillo, Rosalie Spar, and Babs Craven—and Louis Paul and all the pages who fetched materials for me. My gratitude to Dr. Roderick Bladel for turning over to me his important research on theatrical photographers is boundless. I would also like to thank the late Thor Wood, head of the Performing Arts Research Center at Lincoln Center for allowing me special research privileges. It was an act of kindness I cannot forget.

During a prolonged period of research, I ranged far and wide across the country looking for information and illustrations and called upon the personnel and resources of many collections, notably: Dr. Jeanne Newlin and Martha Mahard at the Harvard Theatre Collection; Kathleen Gee of the University of Texas Art Collections; Dr. William Crain of the Hoblitzelle Theatre Collection at the same institution; Louis Rachow, former Librarian of the Hampden-Booth Library of The Players, in New York City; and the staff of the Library of Congress, Prints and Photographs Division.

Among the many individuals I approached for special help and information are Joseph Abeles, Arthur Birsh, Louis Botto, Eileen Darby, Lou Dunetz, Richard Flint, Al Hirschfeld, Alix Jeffry, Carolyn Klein, Hobe Morrison, Sam Norkin, Philip Pocock, Roger Puckett, Harvey Sabinson, Vincent Sardi, Martha Swope, and the late Bernard Simon. I could not have written the book or assembled the illustrations without their contributions. To all of them, my thanks.

If I have a second home away from home, it is the headquarters of Harry N. Abrams, Inc., on lower Fifth Avenue. There resides my extended family in the form of Margaret Kaplan, Executive Editor and friend *extraordinaire;* John Crowley, my dynamic and inspired photographic editor; and Ellyn Allison, whose unfailing good sense and good humor more than make up for those daunting little slips that she attaches to my manuscripts in her role as text editor. To them and to the talented designer of this book, Bob McKee, I owe more than thanks: I owe them the joy of publication, a feeling like no other.

Posters

S ince theater has always been an art in search of an audience—the larger the better—it has (except in rare instances) always needed to advertise its wares. When theatrical performances were part of national ritual or public festivals, as in ancient Greece and Rome, the usual public announcements inscribed on walls were probably rendered superfluous by the commotion created while the immense outdoor theaters were put in order for the show. In later eras, the town crier was assigned the task of announcing performances to an audience so overwhelmingly illiterate that a written bulletin would have been useless. Even the invention of the printing press did not immediately simplify the theater manager's task of advertising upcoming productions. Printing was expensive and audiences still could not read. In America, where the first London touring companies arrived in the mid-eighteenth century, the problem was compounded by a deep-rooted and widespread disapproval of actors and theaters. But by the end of the nineteenth century, liberated by the forces of materialism, capitalism, education, and secularization, the theater found itself free to advertise in as blatant and noisy a style as it wanted—and it did.

The theatrical poster flourished in the nineteenth century because technology had advanced sufficiently to make possible the mass production of cheap printed materials and because there existed a literate public affluent enough to be able to purchase tickets on impulse or on a regular basis with some degree of frequency. Advertising has become the hallmark of an affluent society, existing only when the banquet table is full and varied. When there is only one show in town, the producer can afford to keep his advertising money in his pocket; now as then, when the circus, the Chautauqua lecturer, the vaudeville troupe, and the *East Lynne* traveling show come to town to compete with his repertory company, he pulls the money out of his pocket to

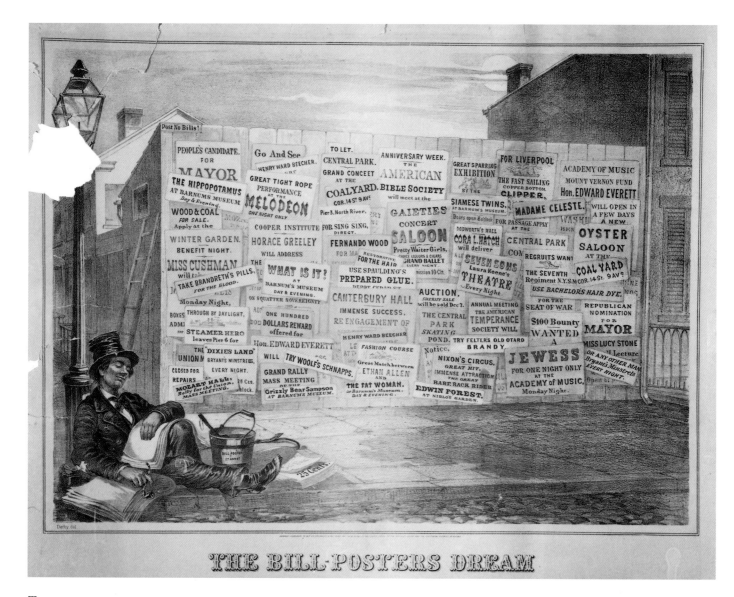

THE BILL-POSTERS DREAM

To a billposter the sight of a blank wall is a nightmare. This mid-nineteenth-century "sniper" slumbers blissfully, paste pot beside him, after his day's work covering a fence with paper advertising everything from a sermon by clergyman Henry Ward Beecher to the hippopotamus at Barnum's Museum. The theater is represented by posters for Charlotte Cushman, Edwin Forrest, Madame Celeste, Bryant's Minstrels, *The Jewess,* and Nixon's Circus, scattered among political announcements and advertisements for wood and coal, concerts, and lectures by Horace Greeley and Edward Everett, among others. Engraving by Derby, 1862

make sure that the citizens do not forget the glories of the performance at the Orpheum. The poster became the best and least expensive way to accomplish his purpose.

There is some confusion about what constitutes a poster. From the mid-eighteenth century onward, something that looks to the modern eye like a small poster was tacked in the doorway of theaters or sold for a penny or two to ticket holders. It was actually a letterpress program, measuring from a few inches in length and width to as much as 7 by 22 inches, giving in varying type and sizes the names of the play and the performers, the day of performance, the name of the theater, and sometimes (but not often enough) the date. These handbills were roughly printed on cheap paper and so heavily inked that the black of the type frequently bled through to the reverse. Later, a rough woodcut illustration of a scene or a star or a decorative symbol might be added to make them more attractive or provocative. The next step, introduced by 1820, was the technique of lithography. This type of printing, from acid-etching on stone, was reserved for more "serious" publications—sheet-music covers and decorative pictures, for example—until later in the nineteenth century.

If he were alive today, H. A. Ogden would be classified as a commercial artist, but during his own time, he worked frequently as a so-called sketch artist. Before the invention of photogravure (which was the first method of reproducing photographs cheaply and efficiently as printed pictures), it was the job of the sketch artist to make drawings of performers, which would then accompany or become the basis for magazine and newspaper articles and posters. One of the Ogden's favorite subjects was the great Edwin Booth. These incomplete but charming drawings of Booth and his company at a rehearsal of *Hamlet* in 1871 may later have been transformed by Ogden into finished works that he offered for sale to a poster printer or a periodical

There is nothing subtle about this poster advertisement of 1877 for Lydia Thompson's production at the Eagle Theatre in Manhattan. It is written in superlatives and printed for the most part in bold type. She is the Queen of Burlesque, her company is famous, the scenery is new and beautiful, and the costumes are both new and magnificent, befitting the brilliant cast. Although effective in its day, the typographic poster was replaced in the last decades of the nineteenth century by the pictorial poster, usually in color

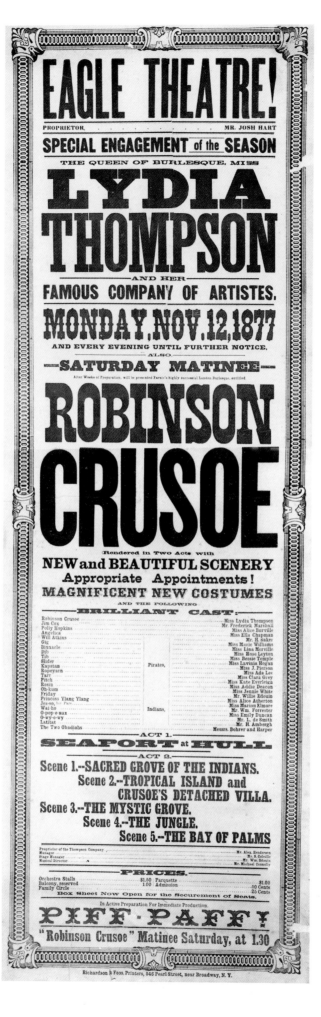

A true poster is never smaller than 14 by 22 inches overall (including the unprinted border), or approximately one-quarter of a "sheet," the standard measurement for which is about 28 by 42 inches, the size of the bed of the printing press throughout most of the nineteenth century and early twentieth century. Posters also come in multiples of sheets, the most common today being the three-sheet format, measuring approximately 42 by 84 inches, less the trim. But posters have filled as many as one hundred sheets. The common billboard size is now thirty sheets, although for many years it was twenty-four sheets. In the trade and among press agents, posters and other types of printed theatrical advertisements were spoken of for many years as "show paper."

Of slightly heavier weight than newsprint, the paper on which one-sheet and multiple-sheet posters were and continue to be printed is manufactured from wood pulp. Unless protected, the poster is destined to a short life. It was and is still pasted illegally on every available free surface, including the fences put around construction sites (an activity called "sniping"), but is

Costumes were such an important part of *The Black Crook,* a landmark musical production that opened at Niblo's Garden in New York in 1866 and held the boards for sixteen months, that this poster for the show was devoted exclusively to drawings of them. F. Mayer & Co. Lithographers, Fulton Street, New York

A wealth of information is revealed in this late-1860s poster for *Dot* at Crosby's Opera House, but the year of the performance is not included among the facts. The job printer crowded at least twelve different typefaces in the smaller than usual, 24-by-9-inch advertisement and also provided a small woodcut in an attempt to give it a distinctive look. C. D. Hess & Co., managers of the Chicago theater, have lured an audience with a list of performers, a description of five dramatic tableaux, previews of coming attractions (*The Flying Scud*), a gratuitous self-critique ("An Excellent Performance"), and the fact that the Friday evening show would be a benefit for the actor John E. Owens

Opposite:

Edward Harrigan, one of the most beloved performers of the last quarter of the nineteenth century, frequently revived his old repertory. This lithographed poster simply shows him in a characteristic pose. H. A. Thomas, Litho. Studio, 30 by 19½ inches

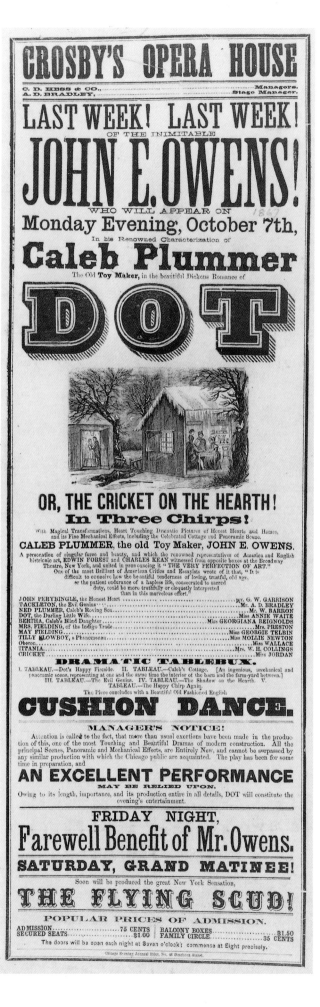

EDWARD HARRIGAN
IN HIS ORIGINAL CREATION "OLD LAVENDER".

In the late nineteenth century, the Philadelphia Ledger Printing Company issued a book that has since become a special kind of historical document. It contains numbered "cuts" of posters for popular shows like *East Lynne* (cut 440 is shown here). The sampler served the useful purpose in its own day of advertising the printing company's wares to advance men, who were hired to publicize traveling shows before their arrival in towns across America. Today it is a source of fascination for social and theatrical historians, who can find in the poster cuts a wealth of information about fashions in dress and gesture and about styles and innovations in scenic design also hung legitimately in spaces within airports, railway stations, and public walls, for a fee. The practice harks back to the late nineteenth century, when, for the privilege of pasting a broadside to his barn, the circus bill-poster gave a farmer and his family free tickets to the show.

Early in the nineteenth century, the circus made the first and most effective use of the poster. Because it was a traveling show, an "advance man" had to herald its coming. By placing posters about the town and villages on its route, he generated a considerable head of steam before the circus arrived for its traditional parade of clowns and menagerie down Main Street. Circus posters were printed from cuts made at first in basswood or mahogany; later, in the 1840s, the American artist Joseph Morse made his cuts in pine, which decreased the cost significantly. He also began pulling posters in several colors, using a block of wood for each color in the composition. Although they were crude in design and concept, they were eye-catching enough to accomplish their job of getting people into the circus tent.

It has been suggested that one of Morse's multicolored posters put up in the early 1860s by the traveling Hawes and Cushing Circus in England arrested the attention of Jules Chéret, who was working in that country at the time as a lithographer. After he returned to Paris in 1867, Chéret began designing colorful posters for circuses, music halls, and shops. Liberated from the woodcut technique, with its inherent restrictions as to sheet size, Chéret was able to produce posters in a range of dimensions. Chéret's lithographic posters became the rage of Paris, and some of the finest artists in France (notably the Post-Impressionists) were soon creating posters advertising everything under the Parisian sun.

M. B. Leavitt, a theatrical entrepreneur, took credit in his autobiography for introducing Continental lithographed posters in America, in 1872. According to his account, while on a trip to Europe, Leavitt bought a large supply of single-color pictorial lithographs, which he later used for the tours of his shows in America. They caused a lively sensation and created a demand for a more sophisticated type of show paper in the American theater. By the end of the decade, lithographed posters had supplanted the woodcuts, and a new era in American postermaking was launched.

By the late 1870s, show business was beginning to become a far-flung enterprise as "Tom shows" (fanciful dramatizations of *Uncle Tom's Cabin*), popular melodramas, and mistrelsy crisscrossed the country. With theatrical activity booming, the demand for show paper was so great that printing houses sprang up coast to coast to satisfy it, but the largest companies were in the midwest, mainly in Ohio, roughly equidistant from the two greatest theater markets, New York and Chicago. On a local level, show paper was produced by the so-called job printers, who made use of the idle presses before and after editions of the local newspapers were printed.

In the late nineteenth century, soft zinc plates that could be rolled around the rotary presses replaced the slabs of limestone originally used in the lithographic process. During the early years of lithography, it was possible to pull one hundred sheets in an hour, but the new equipment made the same feat possible in a minute. Because the most popular plays were constantly on tour, posters advertising them were run off in quantity and warehoused, awaiting orders from local theaters and managers, who could insert the appropriate names, dates of performance,

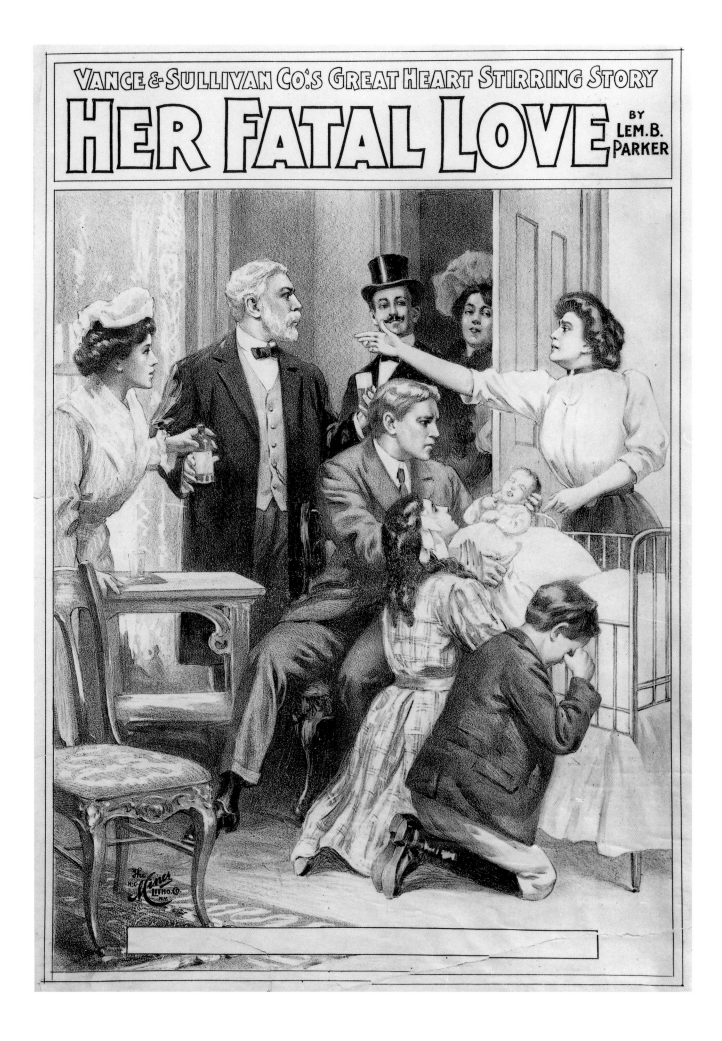

and other pertinent information as "slugs" at the bottom of the sheets. Printers even kept miniature samples called "cuts" on hand so that press agents and advance men could leaf through them quickly and choose what they needed. The job printers and the lithography houses were able to deliver stockpiled show paper to their clients within a day after receiving an order. Occasionally, a job printer overstepped the bounds of business ethics. Rumor had it that the owner of one of New York's prominent dailies refused to publish information about a production or a star unless he got the contract for the show paper in the newspaper's job-printing office.

The Strobridge Lithographing Company, of Cincinnati, Ohio, preeminent among the poster printers because of the high quality and excellent design of its work, became the hub of the show-paper printing business for about fifty years. The company had its origin in an engraving shop set up by Elijah C. Middleton in 1847. The first of the Strobridges joined the firm seven years later, and eventually the family took over the company, changing its name to theirs in 1880. In its formative years, Strobridge had two major assets: Matt Morgan, the company's principal designer, and A. A. Stewart, its supersalesman, whose efforts brought hundreds of thousands of dollars worth of theatrical business into the firm each year. The company was also unusually canny in paying these men handsomely to keep them on board and in maintaining such high standards that their posters were referred to as the Rembrandts of the industry. (M. B. Leavitt reported that he took a number of their posters to Europe, where they created an immediate sensation.) The company survived two disastrous fires and, in 1912, the death of Stewart, who went down with the *Titanic*. A number of Strobridge's competitors attempted to control the printing industry by creating a monopoly, but Strobridge's held on and lived to celebrate its centennial. Before it went out of business, the company had manufactured every kind of commercial paper from calendars to counter displays, and samples of its products have drifted into permanent collections in museums, libraries, and historical societies throughout the country.

Matt Morgan led a somewhat checkered existence both in the theater and in publishing before he joined Strobridge's in 1879. Born in Lambeth, England, in 1836, he was apprenticed at the age of seventeen to scene painters in the London theaters. Four years later, he joined the staff of the *Illustrated London News* as a staff sketch artist and then drew caricatures, before returning to scene painting at Covent Garden. At that time, Frank Leslie was looking for a caricaturist to challenge the dominance of Thomas Nast at *Harper's Weekly*, and in 1871 he persuaded Morgan to come to New York to work for him on *Frank Leslie's Illustrated Weekly*. But Morgan did not succeed in topping Nast. He returned to scene painting and even tried theatrical management, before receiving the offer from Strobridge's. Although most poster designers remained anonymous employees of their companies, Morgan was allowed to sign a number of his creations. More important was his achievement in training a team of designers to turn out striking, well-executed circus and theatrical posters on a consistent basis. One of his artists, Harry Ogden, was assigned to sketch scenes and stars from life and send them from New York to Cincinnati so that they could be worked into softly colored poster designs. By the time he left

Undoubtedly *Her Fatal Love* and the graphic poster that promoted it were intended to appeal to unsophisticated matinee ladies everywhere in America. Many such nineteenth-century melodramas never made it to Broadway. They can be considered the spiritual ancestors of the soap operas of radio and television. H. C. Miner Litho. Co., New York

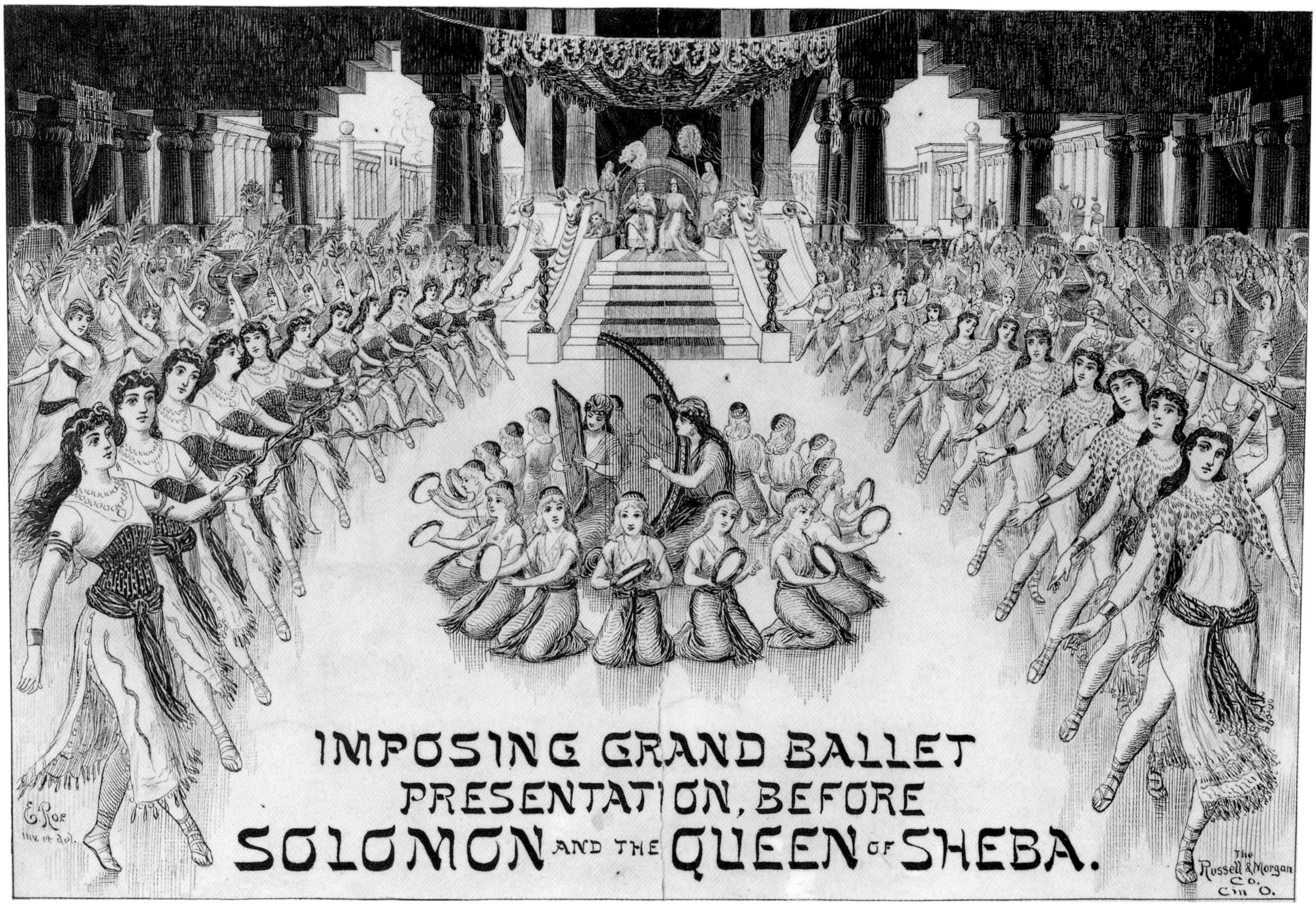

IMPOSING GRAND BALLET
PRESENTATION, BEFORE
SOLOMON AND THE QUEEN OF SHEBA.
E. Roe
The Russell & Morgan Co. Cin O.

In the late nineteenth century, the Russell and Morgan Company of Cincinnati hired E. Rothengatter ("E. Roe") to design its posters. Like Matt Morgan at Strobridge, the artist was allowed to sign his work. Roe's design shown here, a typically overwrought picture-poster of the period, displays, it seems safe to say, an unprecedented amount of female pulchritude

Opposite:

Although *Tea for Three* (1918) ran for a year (and even played an extra Christmas matinee), its history ended with the three hundredth performance. But the poster lives on as an example of what happened to design in the early years of the twentieth century. Gone were the graphic pictorial posters of the previous era, and in their place came simplified, often whimsical examples of the art. H. C. Miner Litho. Co., New York, 42 by 28 inches

Strobridge's, Morgan had made an indelible mark not only on the company but on the art of the poster in America.

Before Morgan, theatrical posters often depicted a sensational scene from a play, complete with a climactic line of dialogue. The actors often looked nondescript, the coloring veered toward the garish, and the draftsmanship was of poor quality. More often than not, the artist chose a photograph from the New York run of the play, transformed it into a rough sketch, and enlarged and sometimes colored it. Since the manager or producer exercised very little control over the end product, the responsibility for creating the poster resided with the printer. But the nineteenth-century theater poster needs no apology. Noisy, but not violent (to paraphrase theater critic Brander Matthews), it accomplished its purpose, advertising the theater's plentiful offerings like "a brass band that plays in tune." Occasionally, one or another of them slipped into art; often a top manager like Charles Frohman or Lester Wallack insisted on something out of the ordinary and engaged a recognized artist to design a poster for him; but, for the most part, the nineteenth-century poster did not aspire to high art and was never intended to survive the sun, wind, rain, sleet, and snow of its ultimate outdoor environment.

By 1920, printing show paper could no longer sustain an individual business, let alone an entire industry. Companies like Strobridge's had already diversified when the demand for theatrical posters and advertisements began to shrink, along with the number of shows on the road. Theatrical activity was centered more and more in New York City, and most of the industries that depended on it for support relocated to New York addresses. The company that arose to succeed Strobridge's was the Artcraft Lithograph and Printing Company, founded in 1922 in lower Manhattan by Samuel Golden and continuing today in business under the aegis of his son Allen Golden. For about forty years, Artcraft dominated the field, printing for thousands of shows, but in recent years it has surrendered its hegemony to Scoop Printing Company, a New York printing house established in 1958 by Sid Cooper. Though Scoop works through and with advertising agencies rather than directly with producers or press agents, the company performs the same traditional functions of printing, stocking, and shipping posters, utilizing the latest in printing technology and transportation.

Today most posters are printed by offset, a photographic process that has revolutionized the printing industry in the last twenty-five years. Completed, "camera-ready" artwork is given to the printer, who then photographs it and transfers the film onto printing plates (using a different plate or "separation" for each color). Lithography has been adapted to the offset process and yields a finer product, as does serigraphy (silk-screening), which is the product of human hands, making it increasingly expensive but the finest and most artful of all. The two most popular poster types are the 14-by-22-inch window card (the old quarter-sheet), printed on heavy (usually coated) stock and laminated to cardboard, and the familiar three-sheet, now printed in two rather than three pieces. Posters are still printed in quantity and stocked for shipment. If necessary, they can be flown to their destination in time to be posted the following day in the theater where the show will open, in ticket offices, on fences, in subway and bus stations, in railway and air terminals, and in all the other traditional locations.

Although the Theatre Guild production of S. N. Behrman's play *Meteor* was a failure during the 1929–30 season, the attractive poster was up to the Guild's usual high standards. Designed by F. M. Walts, 22 by 14 inches

Opposite:

Basking in its success during the 1927–28 season in New York, the Theatre Guild decided to launch a secondary company and tour it in *The Guardsman* around the country's boondocks. Heading the troupe were George Gaul and Florence Eldridge, who had played in the Guild's past hits. With a simple change of names, the poster designed by Lee Simonson for the 1924 production in New York was dusted off and sent along with them. Carey & Sons, New York, 22 by 14 inches

Posters today represent thousands of dollars of the producer's irreclaimable money and have to be not only letter-perfect but a fulfillment of all of the conditions specified in the contracts of the writers, performers, director, and designers with the producers. A theatrical publicist's nightmare is a poster error. Harvey Sabinson, one of the most creative Broadway press agents ever, relates in his memoirs a near-catastrophe that brought him to the brink of breakdown. The director of the production on which he was working saw the poster for the play and immediately objected to having his name printed in green while all the others on the poster were in blue. He called forth his contract and read the clause to Sabinson. "Your credit shall appear last, on a separate line on which no other words or names shall appear and shall be in the same boldness

Hilary Knight is one of perhaps a dozen artists who discovered and developed the art of the theater poster in the 1960s. Like his colleagues, Knight varies his style from poster to poster and creates something unique in both spirit and technique for each production for which he designs the identifying visual symbol. In this window card (22 by 14 inches), Knight covered the space with the exuberant figure of the star of *Half a Sixpence* (1965), displaying a notable economy of line and detail. He also deemphasized the credits by boxing them at bottom right. Artcraft Lithograph and Printing Company, New York

Opposite:

Although the Kurt Weill–Bertold Brecht musical, *The Threepenny Opera*, had a seven-year engagement at the Theater de Lys (it opened and closed in 1954 and reopened the following year to complete the run), original window cards of David Stone Martin's striking black-and-white poster are now something of a rarity. The poster set a high standard for Off Broadway productions from the moment it appeared. E. J. Warner Poster Corp., 22 by 14 inches

and prominence of type and at least fifty percent of the size of the largest letter of the billing used for the title of the play or the separate names of not more than two stars, or any credit, whichever is largest, but never less than the credit for the author, whether or not the said author's name is above or below the title." The director was convinced that the color blue was bolder than the color green. Sabinson consulted art experts but was unable to summon up a definite consensus as to the relative boldness of green and blue. When all else failed, he explained his dilemma to the printer at Artcraft, who arrived at a solution. He would print up strips in the correct color with an adhesive on the back, to be pasted over the offending color at a cost of fifty dollars. At the eleventh hour, Sabinson personally pasted the new strips to the first group of posters. Congratulating himself at having saved the producer's dollars and

Opposite:

This was Gilbert Lesser's first try at designing a poster for a Broadway play. It has since passed into history as one of the most stunning modern examples of the genre. The playwright Peter Shaffer, author of *Equus* (1974), described Lesser's technique as "an exquisitely pleasing austerity." His design, all circles and rectangles, has the brutal bite of the play it represents. Scoop Printing Company, New York

Originally printed in three sections, "three-sheet" posters are today printed in two pieces. These large-size advertisements (42 by 84 inches, less the trim) are usually not created until a show has proved its box-office appeal. Very often they contain a favorable comment or two by the critics or list the awards the show has won. During the course of a long run, freshly designed three-sheets are distributed and posted at intervals to stimulate interest in the production. *A Chorus Line*, the record-breaking Broadway musical, has been represented since 1975 by a series of posters that have been designed and redesigned many times to keep abreast of the history of this "singular sensation." Here is an example in the series, featuring a photo montage by Paul Elson and Martha Swope. Scoop Printing Company, New York

the director's face in one inexpensive coup, he proudly announced his ingenious solution to the producer, only to be told: "I couldn't care less. I just fired the son of a bitch."

In the twentieth century, the American theater poster, perhaps in emulation of the European theater poster, has benefited from better and more thoughtful design. The harrowing posters of yore depicting scenes of bloodhounds pursuing poor Eliza and the moustachioed villain chloroforming the unprotected working girl have given way to subtler, more symbolic, and more consciously artistic conceptions. The maturation of the poster coincided, not surprisingly, with the maturation of the theater itself in this country. No institution had greater influence on both than the Theatre Guild, which rose to become the leading commercial avant-garde production group in America, shortly after its founding in 1919. Utilizing the talents of its staff artists and designers, the Guild commissioned exceptionally fine posters of unusual design, filled with forceful and provocative symbols and bold and arresting color. The idea that a poster should reflect, even underscore, the value of a production has endured. Since then, posters have become less literal and more metaphorical and stylized. Color has been used as an element of the design. Recognized artists are engaged by the producer or his advertising agency to reveal the essence of the show in the poster. Paradoxically, the design of theater posters has continued to improve as the impact of live theater on the daily lives of Americans has lessened.

No artist today can earn a living by designing theatrical posters. Occasionally the work of one artist or another will dominate for a season, or a producer may allow one artist's concepts to identify his productions. The association of Joseph Papp and the New York Shakespeare Festival and artist Paul Davis comes to mind. But styles change and tastes vary too rapidly to permit any one artist to remain in the ascendant very long.

Today the poster designer is given a script to read and costume and scenic designs to examine and he may be invited to a rehearsal to meet with the company. He not only looks for inspiration in the play, production, and performers but may delve into history and art. The idea for the pungent poster for the 1954–55 revival of *The Threepenny Opera* came to David Stone Martin only after he had stumbled on the satiric drawings of George Grosz and the protest posters of Frans Masereel. At its best, the poster comes to represent not just the play but the spirit of the production or the concept of the revival. Now more than ever, it becomes part of the history of the play. It is the tangible and very visual evidence that the production has been done in such and such a way at a certain time in history. Intended for a fleeting life, theatrical posters are eagerly collected by aficionados as much for their aesthetic value as for the memories they inspire of a performance.

By toning down the garish colors and paying attention to design and appropriateness, Matt Morgan was able to transform the late nineteenth-century poster into something closer to art. He was one of the few poster designers of the era who was allowed to sign his work. Shown is a signed Morgan poster depicting J. K. "Fritz" Emmet, a deft dialect comedian who in the 1880s was renowned for his "Dutch," or German, act. Strobridge Lithographing Co., Cincinnati

Yesterday's audiences throve on sentimentality. Beginning in 1888, a perennial favorite was *Little Lord Fauntleroy*, based on Frances Hodgson Burnett's immensely popular novel about a poor boy suddenly elevated to life as the grandson of an earl. With little Elsie Leslie playing the child in the original production, the tale became even more popular as a play, evolving into a kind of social document about the English class system. Many posters were printed for the show, each featuring a different scene—the weepier the better. Springer Litho. Co., New York, 28¼ by 21½ inches

The producer M. B. Leavitt maintained that he was the first to introduce chromolithographed posters in the United States. For his road-show revival of *Mazeppa* in the late 1880s, he commissioned this busy and noisy example, reluctant, apparently, to leave much to the imagination of rustic audiences. Enquirer Job Printing Co., Cincinnati, 27 by 41 inches

Mama and Papa Cohan announced proudly the talents of their children George and Josie on this poster for the production of *Widow McCann's Trip*, a concoction for the entire family of mirth makers. It went on the road with them in 1891. Great Western Litho Co., St. Louis, 21 by 28½ inches

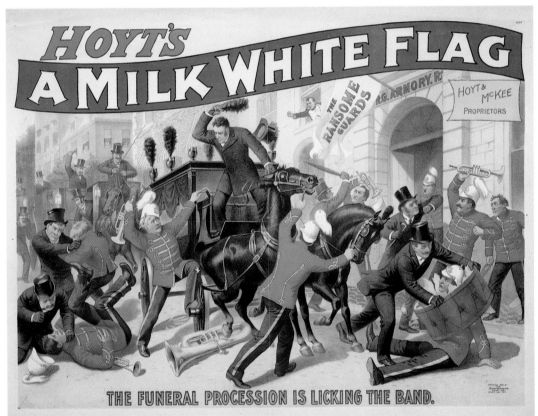

Charles Hoyt's genius for farcical situations emanates from this poster for *A Milk White Flag*, of 1894. A Strobridge creation, it typically depicts a scene from the play—the more boisterous the better. Strobridge Lithographing Co., Cincinnati and New York, 28½ by 39 inches

This striking poster for Joseph Hart's Specialty Company documents the first major change in the American theater in the late nineteenth century. Replacing the old resident stock companies, traveling combination companies (this one is called a specialty company) traversed the country with a star, scenery, and costumes playing a repertory of shows. Since the star (Charles T. Aldrich, in this case) was the drawing card, the poster became an advertisement for him (or her). Counian Litho. Co., Buffalo, New York, 42 by 28½ inches

One of producer William A. Brady's greatest successes was *Way Down East*. After its long Broadway run in 1898, the show played on the road for years, at each stop heralded by a homey poster depicting a sentimental moment in the play. *Way Down East* enjoyed a second incarnation in a movie made by D. W. Griffith and starring Lillian Gish as the waiflike heroine. 29¼ by 19½ inches

Far left:

If anyone remembers Marie Dressler today, it is as a highly successful character actress in the movies. But before that she was the toast of Broadway: a leading lady and a charming soubrette. This poster of Dressler in *Miss Prinnt* (1900) reveals the vivacity that enraptured New York audiences. 25½ by 16¾ inches

Left:

Although Henry C. Miner made a name and a living from his printing business, he also aspired to theater management and politics. Reflecting both professional pride and his love for the stage, this stunning poster portrays Julian Eltinge, the greatest female impersonator of his day, in *Cousin Lucy*, his starring vehicle of 1915. H. C. Miner Litho. Co., New York, 35 by 23½ inches

A number of plays produced about the turn of the century never made it to Broadway—for good reason. Such a one was *Tennessee Tess*, a melodrama that thrilled unsophisticated audiences across the land about 1900 but would have failed to please worldly New Yorkers. This poster, designed by Otto Lambert Grever, shows one of the crucial moments in the play, leaving nothing to the imagination. Printed by H. C. Miner Litho. Co., New York, 28 by 39½ inches

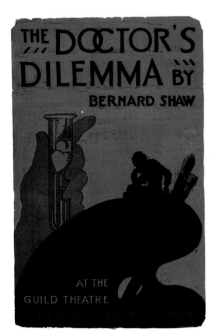

Two advertisements of Theatre Guild productions reveal the complete change in poster art for which the Guild was largely responsible in the 1920s and 1930s. Each window-card-size announcement was individually designed to capture the essence of the play, and each was signed by its creator. Lee Simonson, a Guild board director and principal scenic designer for the company, frequently designed posters in addition to his other chores. Shown above is Simonson's 1927 poster for *The Doctor's Dilemma* (printed by Carey & Sons, New York, 22 by 14 inches). Shown at right is Franklin Hughes's 1930 poster for *Roar China* (printed by the Golden Press, 22 by 14 inches)

In 1935, President Roosevelt's Works Progress Administration established a special unit, the Federal Theatre Project, to take unemployed theatrical folk off the welfare rolls. A sister unit, the Federal Art Project, was often enlisted to design posters for FTP productions. One of the most interesting results of the cooperation between these two agencies is this window card for the 1938 production of *Androcles and the Lion*

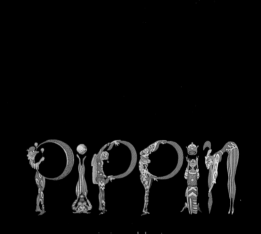

PACIFIC OVERTURES

Pacific Overtures

THE SHUBERT ORGANIZATION
McCANN & NUGENT
present

PACIFIC OVERTURES

Music & Lyrics by   Book by
STEPHEN SONDHEIM   JOHN WEIDMAN

Additional Material by
HUGH WHEELER

Originally Directed and Produced by
HAROLD PRINCE

Scenery Designed by   Lighting Designed by   Costumes Designed by   Additional Costumes by
JAMES MORGAN   MARY JO DONDLINGER   MARK PASSERELL   EIKO YAMAGUCHI

Musical Director   Orchestrations by   Originally Choreographed by   Choreographer
ERIC STERN   JAMES STENBORG   PATRICIA BIRCH   JANET WATSON

Directed by
FRAN SOEDER

This production based on the March, 1984 York Theatre Company production,
Janet Hayes Walker, Producing Director.

In recent years, scene designers have often been commissioned to create posters for the productions with which they are associated. Here is a striking example by Tony Walton, who is among the leaders in the profession today. It is a window placard for the big and splashy 1972 musical *Pippin.* Artcraft Lithograph and Printing Company, New York

Frank Verlizzo ("Fraver"), the award-winning creator of theatrical posters, observed that a poster can have a life of its own. One example he designed for a flop show can still be found in theater memorabilia stores. He regards posters as the advance guard of theatrical production—they must establish an image "to sell the show even before the show starts." The Bronx-born artist believes that today's producers are more concerned that a poster be "an actual artistic extension of a production" and are especially careful in their selection of a design. Verlizzo enjoys working up designs for Stephen Sondheim's musicals. For *Pacific Overtures* (1976), he blended Japanese and American symbols (a samurai warrior and the American Stars and Stripes) to reflect the message of the musical and its bold colors. Scoop Printing Company, New York

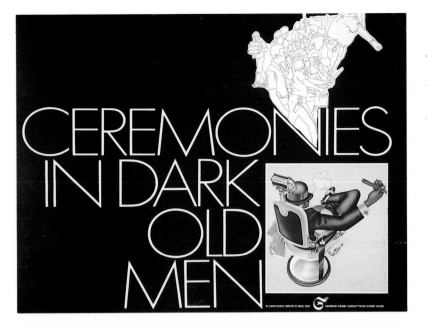

With Broadway providing the inspiration, many of the Off Broadway and regional theaters established in the 1950s and 1960s eventually became prosperous and sophisticated enough to produce posters rivaling (and sometimes surpassing) in quality of design some of the commercial theater's best examples. Shown is a poster for *Ceremonies in Dark Old Men*, produced in 1979 at the Tyrone Guthrie Theatre, designed by Nordahl for the Minnesota Theatre Company

Paul Davis's poster for Joseph Papp's New York Public Theater production of *The Mystery of Edwin Drood* (1985) makes no attempt to disguise the sex of the leading player. Despite the cigar, she is obviously an actress dressed as a man. It is also obvious that *Edwin Drood* is a musical. The design represents a departure from Davis's usually understated Public Theater posters in that it lists everybody associated with the production for its move to Broadway. Since 1975, Davis has been designer for Joseph Papp's productions, and his posters have given the Public Theater a recognizable public image. Davis attended the School of Visual Arts in New York and then drifted into commercial art and illustration before signing on with the Public Theater. He believes that posters are street art. "They're designed to be bolder and stronger and louder. There's something very gritty and emotional that just doesn't exist in other work. That's what the theater is often about—that kind of intensity. I try to get into the posters that raw, emotional quality." Scoop Printing Company, New York

To explain the evolution of James McMullan's poster for the revival of *Anything Goes* (1987), *Print Magazine* ran a series of illustrations with their article. McMullan's original idea was to depict the musical's young lovers, but later a decision was made to focus on the show's most arresting character, Reno Sweeney, the tough nightclub singer. The artist then posed a friend on the Staten Island ferry for a series of reference photographs before tackling the design, which passed through a series of refinements before the final version made it into print. Printed by Triumph Productions. © James McMullan

In the glory days of Broadway, producers would rent billboards the length and breadth of the country to advertise their latest New York success, but times have changed and with them the techniques of advertising. Whereas in the past the posters were printed in various sheet sizes to fit standard billboards, today it is more economical to have posters reproduced as paintings on the sides of buildings. In 1988 the skilled sign painters of the Van Wagner Company reproduced three posters for the Lincoln Center Theater Company productions of *Sarafina!*, *Speed-the-Plow*, and *Anything Goes* on a 57-by-121-foot space atop a building in the Times Square theater district

Today, posters are printed as small window cards or in the much larger and bolder "three-sheet" size. The larger posters are generally destined for public places like airports and bus and train terminals, but they are also a necessary part of the scenery of Shubert Alley, which runs through the block from West Forty-fourth Street to West Forty-fifth Street, in the heart of the theater district in New York. From the bright red of *42nd Street* to the deep black of *Cats*, these posters immediately catch the eye and help to lure prospective ticket buyers into the nearby box offices

One of the busiest of the Broadway poster designers is Doug Johnson, who started in the field more than fifteen years ago. A Canadian by birth and training, he first worked for the Chelsea Theatre Group when they were located in Brooklyn. He was soon not only designing their posters but handling their advertising and promotion, eventually joining the production staff. When Chelsea languished, he became part of a group known as Dodger Productions that engaged actively in bringing musical shows to Broadway and Off Broadway. He has used a variety of styles, from the frankly pictorial to the boldly typographical. Shown is his powerful advertisement for *The Gospel at Colonus,* a short-lived musical of 1988. When he has been producer as well as designer for a show, enjoying a rare freedom, he has deemphasized the production credits to the point of partially obscuring them, as is evident in this example. Printed by Robert Silverman, New York

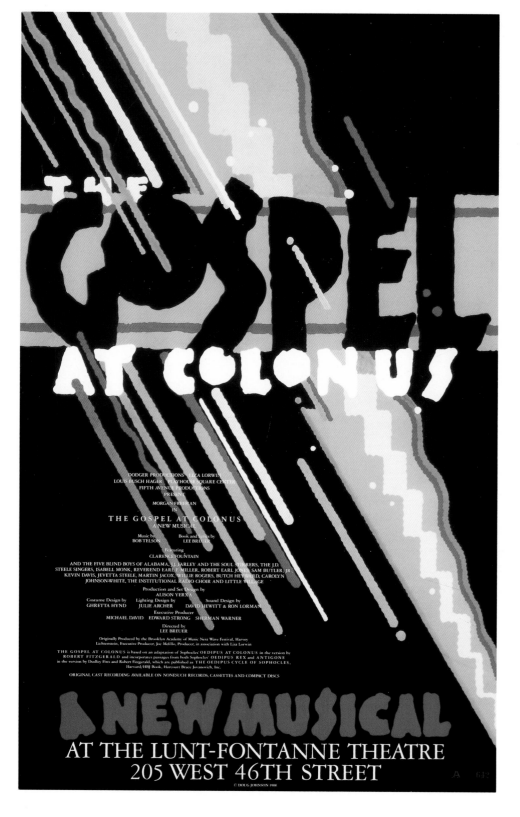

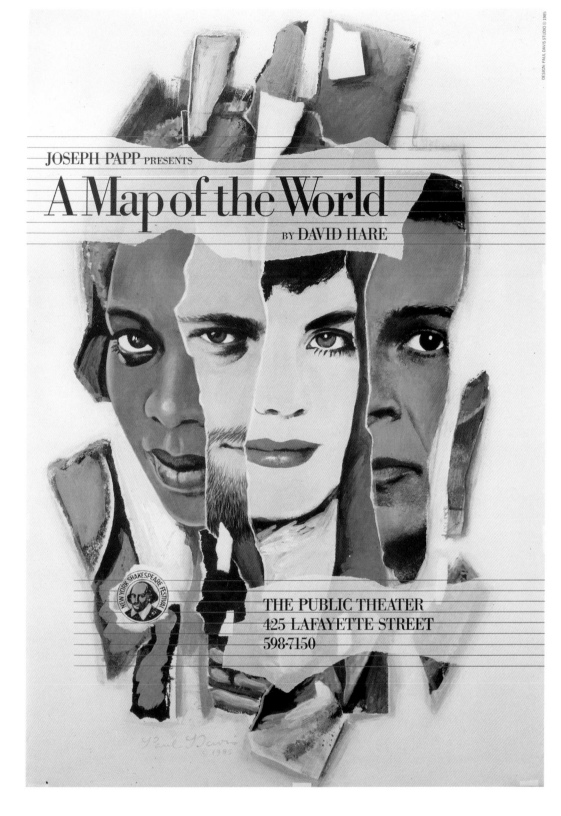

The typical Paul Davis poster for the productions of the New York Shakespeare Festival features a large and startling image that engulfs the entire sheet. The name of the play, the playwright, and the theater are prominent, but no other credits are listed. Here shown is the poster designed by Davis for *A Map of the World* by David Hare (1985). Printed by Stevens/Bendes, New York

Photographs

P hotography has profoundly affected the history of the theater in America. Prior to its invention, about the middle of the nineteenth century, the iconography of the theater was woefully sparse. The most successful actors were painted by first-rate artists, but the faces and figures of many major and most minor early players will remain forever unknown to us. Extremely rare are quality pictures of performers and playhouses before 1800. After 1800, when theaters began to gain a place among the most prominent and architecturally attractive buildings in major cities, pictorial records gradually accumulated, providing us with a reasonably good idea of what the American nineteenth-century playhouse looked like, both inside and out.

The fortunes of theatrical publications were advanced significantly by photography. So real, so lifelike, and so useful to the lithographer and engraver did its images prove that they quickly made obsolete the staff artist's sketches of any subject. The photograph was cheap and immediate, and the technology to transfer it from its copper, tin, or paper original to printer's plates was sought almost the day after its invention. Color photography, too, was quickly taken up by the printing industry to enhance the pages of magazines of large circulation and the photogravure sections of newspapers.

The official date of the invention of photography is 1839. In that year the French Chamber of Deputies granted Louis Jacques Mandé Daguerre a government stipend and the exclusive rights to the process that he had developed, later known as daguerreotypy. Daguerre was by profession a designer of stage scenery, one of the most successful of his time. Early in the century, he worked in Paris at both the Opéra and the Ambigu-Comique, a theater known for its productions of sensational melodramas. A master of the trompe l'oeil technique, Daguerre grew famous for his sets, which, according to the critics of the day, were themselves worth the price of admission.

While designing for the theater, Daguerre developed a new kind of popular entertainment, the diorama. Based on an invention of Philip De Loutherbourgh, chief scenic designer under David Garrick at the Drury Lane Theatre in London, the Eidophusikon was a vivid scenic display (without actors) of special effects, such as thunderstorms, fires, erupting volcanoes, and cloud formations, on a small stage. Daguerre created dioramas of cities and of historical scenes,

In 1844, twenty-one-year-old da-guerreotypist Mathew B. Brady opened his first studio (with the backing of inventor Samuel F. B. Morse) on the corner of Broadway and Fulton Street, then New York's busiest cross-road. In 1861 Brady's success as a portrait photographer and the northward drift of the city led him to open up expanded and sumptuous quarters at Broadway and Tenth Street. *Frank Leslie's Illustrated Weekly* duly recorded the move in its pages. Here flocked illustrious Americans from all walks of life, including the theater, to have their like-nesses fixed on silver-coated copper plates

making them appear to move with the help of shifting transparent screens, imaginative lighting, and false perspective. Dioramas became the rage of Paris and the other principal cities of the Western world.

During the 1820s, Daguerre conducted experiments to capture perfect optical images on paper, canvas, or other ground. As an artist and draftsman, he had worked with the camera obscura, a mechanical device used for centuries to project accurate images on paper. As a scene painter, he was accustomed to add light-reflecting chemicals to his paints to enhance the luminosity of his stage sets and dioramas. Intuiting a profitable relationship between the camera obscura and light-sensitive chemicals, Daguerre was deep in serious experimentation when, in 1827, he discovered that a fellow Frenchman, Joseph-Nicéphore Niépce had learned to set photographic images on silver-coated copper plates. After four years of cagey correspondence, the two inventors finally agreed to pool their findings. In 1833, Niépce died, leaving the field clear for Daguerre.

Although Niépce and Daguerre are credited with the invention of proto-photography, in fact they merely won the race for recognition. During the 1820s and 1830s, experiments along lines similar to theirs were being conducted throughout the Western world. William Henry Fox Talbot, an English artist-scientist, had discovered a method of fixing photographic images on paper as early as 1834. By 1840 he had even developed a prototype of the modern-day negative-positive process. But Talbot's calotypes and Talbotypes never supplanted the daguerreotype on the commercial market.

As daguerreotype studios began springing up in large cities, actors and actresses, like a host of Americans in other walks of life, went to have their likenesses recorded on copper plates.

But it was not until mid-century, with the American tour of the popular Swedish coloratura Jenny Lind, that the publicity value of the photograph was fully understood by the theater people, who for a decade at least continued to be nurtured by a spirit more of legend than of legacy.

At the time of Madame Lind's arrival, it was the practice of many prominent daguerreotypists to sell pictures of celebrities. It worked this way: a celebrity was invited to sit for a picture, and a number of plates were made at this sitting. Since each exposure resulted in only one plate, each daguerreotype was essentially an original. The sitter was invited to select one or more of the plates for his or her personal use and the rest of the copperplate portraits were placed on sale in the daguerreotypist's gallery. Depending upon the importance or attractiveness of the celebrity, the plates might fetch from one to several dollars.

Madame Lind's manager, the redoubtable publicist P. T. Barnum, had created such a furor of public anticipation that her appearances might have proved a fiasco had she not been endowed with genuine gifts. But the public was not duped, it was delighted. Wherever she traveled, her stop always included a trip to the leading daguerreotypist. Her head and neck would be clamped in a brace and she was asked to remain immobile for as long as she had patience or time. In New York, she posed for Mathew Brady; one of his Lind daguerreotypes later received wide circulation when it was made into a lithograph by François D'Avignon. An original daguerreotype of the singer sold for at least five dollars, perhaps for as much as twenty-five dollars, and without doubt the possession of one of the plates lent its owner uncommon status. As a result, interest in collecting portraits of other notables grew apace. When the daguerreotype was supplanted by the paper photograph, collecting likenesses became (as it has since remained) a universal mania.

Actors and actresses gradually recognized the publicity value of their portrait photographs and became eager to comply with any request for a picture. The legendary Sarah Bernhardt is said to have been one of the very few stars who received a fee for posing. Most got nothing more than a few keepsakes for themselves. Photographers tried to keep their bins filled with pictures of performers in their roles, since they constituted an excellent source of income. In the 1870s *Anthony's Photographic Bulletin,* one of the earliest photographic trade journals, advertised supplies of "beautiful photographs of celebrities as studies," at $1.50 per dozen for the small "card" size and $4.50 per dozen for the larger, "cabinet" size. José Maria Mora, one of the leading theatrical photographers of the late 1870s, reported that in one year he had sold more than three hundred thousand pictures of celebrities for a total of ninety thousand dollars!

The early professional photographers enjoyed working with performers. Actors were not inhibited by the camera and they responded well to direction. They came equipped with a change of costume and, according to one photographer, actresses always remembered "to bring with them a collection of toilet paraphernalia, by which we can arrange and decorate them at pleasure, throwing up any points of beauty and hiding unwelcome blemishes."

To make their pictures more interesting, the leading celebrity photographers provided backgrounds for their clientele. Screens, fireplaces, columns, window units, steps, balustrades,

One of Mathew Brady's most lucrative ideas was to sell his daguerreotypes of Americans prominent in all professions to commercial lithographers for mass distribution in printed form. François D'Avignon took Brady's portrait of the singer Jenny Lind (right), made a transfer lithograph (the image was reversed during the process) and published it in 1850 (below)

The arrival of Junius Brutus Booth on American shores in 1821 and his decision to remain not only marked the birth of a dynasty of actors and actor-managers but also caused a change in American acting styles. A dynamic and frequently unrestrained performer, J. B. Booth was capable of electrifying his audiences. He was also a consummate professional in his best moments and raised the standards of performance. Shown here is Booth as Hamlet in an ambrotype, an early photograph that briefly succeeded the daguerreotype. The image was fixed on a glass plate, which was then lacquered in black on the reverse to reveal the subject. The black paint frequently scratched, chipped, or peeled, as has the original of this reproduction

One could hardly guess from this demure daguerreotype, probably of the 1850s, that the subject was the female sex symbol of her age. Born about 1818, Lola Montez carved a notorious reputation on two continents and enjoyed a brief stage career performing her Spider Dance and playing herself. She had a legion of admirers, despite her notable lack of talent as an actress and dancer

Because they scratch easily, small daguerreotypes, such as this four-inch-square portrait of the actor Lester Wallack, were generally encased in plush boxes and surrounded by elaborate frames. Wallack was proprietor in the last half of the nineteenth century of one of the most famous theaters in New York. His good looks coupled with his dramatic talents made him one of the most popular performers of the nineteenth century

Gabriel Harrison was a man of many talents. An actor, playwright, theater manager, and painter, he developed a passion for daguerreotypy when it was introduced in America in 1839 and learned the process quickly. Closely acquainted with the great theatrical and literary figures of his day, he photographed them for the next twenty years, turning some of the portraits into paintings. Here shown is Harrison's early paper photograph of his friend Edwin Forrest, a heroic actor of the nineteenth century, as Brutus

rocks, and painted backdrops were arranged for greatest effect behind or around them. Napoleon Sarony's photographic bric-a-brac acquired such cachet that he began to manufacture it for sale around the country. The "Sarony curtain" became stock-in-trade for the provincial photographer.

Two sizes of photographs were particularly favored by the public. The first was the *carte-de-visite*, the card photograph, measuring on its cardboard mount about 4 inches high by 2½ inches wide. The second was the cabinet photograph, measuring with its mount approximately 6¼ by 4½ inches. The card photograph, patented in France by Adolphe-Eugène Disderi in 1854, was popularized, as the legend goes, by the duke of Parma, whose personal calling cards bore his likeness. When it reached America, in 1860, the card photograph became an instantaneous success. Since it could be produced cheaply in great quantities, it was adopted as an advertising and promotional device and was often given away free of charge, like the baseball card today. Celebrity pictures in this size were in greatest demand, and millions of them, advertising everything from soap to cigarettes to candy, flooded the country.

Just when the card photograph was beginning to decline in popularity, the cabinet photograph arrived from England. Its name, never satisfactorily explained, may well have been derived from the Italian *gabbinetta*, or museum room, where small objects and miniature portraits are displayed. The cabinet format would have been appropriate for display in such a room.

The impact of the photograph on the theater cannot be overemphasized. The theatrical photographer emerged in the late nineteenth century as a manipulator of public taste. From

No well-equipped middle-class home of the late nineteenth century lacked a stereoscope for the delectation of the family. Two photographs made with a double-lens camera—the lenses were set about 2½ inches apart to simulate the distance between the human eyes—were printed side by side. When the double picture was placed in a viewer, the result was an optical illusion of a three-dimensional image. Most stereoscopic pictures were outdoor vistas or panoramic views, but occasionally the best-known performers were the subjects. In this stereoscopic photograph, made in 1863 by E. & H. T. Anthony, the wedding of the midget Tom Thumb and the dwarf Lavinia Warren was recorded for posterity

Entered according to Act of Congress in the year 1863, by E. & H.T. Anthony, in the Clerk's office of the District Court of the U.S, for the So. District of New York.

One of Mathew Brady's competitors was Jeremiah Gurney, a jeweler from Saratoga Springs, who moved to New York so that he could learn daguerreotypy and make it an adjunct of his business. His portraits earned more awards than Brady's, and when the photographic process supplanted daguerreotypy, Gurney's studio became the training ground for many budding photographers. A favorite subject of the photographic corps was the adorable Lotta (actress Charlotte Crabtree), shown here, cigar in hand, in a cabinet photo made in 1868 by J. Gurney & Son

George Rockwood's studio prospered in the early 1860s by producing and marketing by the thousands little *cartes-de-visite*, also called card photographs. While working as a newspaperman in Troy, New York, Rockwood exerted much effort to find a way to transfer photographs to printing plates, and he eventually succeeded in patenting a photoengraving process that revealed shades as well as lines. Shown is a cabinet photograph, made by Rockwood about 1870, of the great actor Edwin Booth

simply wanting a likeness of a favorite performer, the public was coaxed into buying portraits of personalities blessed with attractive faces and figures. Although physical beauty had long been a stage asset, distance and soft lights could always be counted on to lend enchantment to less than perfect features, blemished skin, receding hairlines, or sagging bodies. An actor's talent, too, could overshadow physical imperfections. Photographs, on the other hand, revealed such faults in relentless detail. Soon stars began to emerge in the theatrical firmament with little to recommend them but near-perfect faces and figures—and an elusive, unexplainable photogenic quality. (Later—much later—the motion-picture camera would conjure up creatures whose sole attraction resided in their charismatic images on the silver screen.)

An early case in point is Maud Branscombe. There is hardly a mention of her in the annals of the American stage, and by the 1890s her only appearances were in the Bow Street police court in London, but from the late 1870s to the early 1880s, Maud Branscombe's face was well known throughout America. Her talents were almost nonexistent, but her photographs sold by the hundreds of thousands. She appeared in advertisements, on give-away cards, and in cabinet photographs sold at local galleries. She was the darling of José Maria Mora, who reported to the *Spirit of the Times* that he had sold no fewer than twenty-eight thousand copies of her photographs in 1877. He justified her popularity with a dash of cynicism: "As regards theatrical people, as I have said, fame is altogether subordinate to a picturesque or beautiful face. The

The photograph by Napoleon Sarony (below left) of actresses Kate Claxton and Kitty Blanchard in the 1874 production of *The Two Orphans* appeared in a number of variations on cigar boxes, advertising vehicles of all kinds, and the cover of sheet music from the show (below right), becoming one of the most widely circulated photographs of the late nineteenth century

Bradley & Rulofson's Celebrities.
SAN FRANCISCO, CAL.

By 1880 there was a successful celebrity photographer or photographic studio in every major city in the United States. Bradley & Rulofson's in San Francisco hit upon the novel idea of advertising its wares by cramming the heads of more than one hundred theatrical celebrities into a single cabinet photograph

greatest tragedienne that ever lived will sell less than a mere figurante, providing that the figurante be prepossessing or made to look so." Some years later, a writer in *Vanity Fair* observed that the Branscombe photographs "had taken us in, kidded us, led us around by the ear, wire-tapped us, sold us green goods, handed us an auriferous brick that was not really gold."

Many subsequent eras have produced their "most photographed woman in the world," from Lillian Russell to Marilyn Monroe. To what degree photographic exposure contributed to their vogue can be only casually assessed, but the photograph certainly added a new dimension to the acquisition of stardom. A beautiful or handsome and photogenic face will not guarantee success, but from the dawning of the photographic age in the nineteenth century, stardom has been more difficult to attain without it.

There does not exist any modern equivalent of the mania for collecting celebrity photographs during the 1880s. Every large city had its small shops lined with bins of reproductions at various prices of familiar faces of presidents, politicians, orators, writers and—especially—stage personalities. On the streets, peddlers hawked regenerations of original cabinet photographs, called "newsboys," at five cents a print. Wholesale prices for prime cabinets printed through the silver-albumen process were advertised at twenty dollars per hundred, and for a poorer quality two dollars and fifty cents per hundred. Photographic card advertisements, some as small as postage stamps, were inserted into cigarette, cigar, candy, corset, and soap boxes.

In New York, the photograph shops were clustered around Nassau, William, and John streets, sufficiently far away from the Broadway celebrity photographers, who were listing their wares for nationwide distribution. The popularity of various celebrities was reflected in the sales of their pictures throughout the country. Lillie Langtry suffered a decline in sales, it was reported, when her private life became sullied. Mary Anderson, on the other hand, with an unblemished reputation, continued to sell well. Lillian Russell's sales shot ahead of all others within the space of twelve months and she remained a best-seller for years. When Bernhardt traveled the country on her famous American tours, the sales of her pictures peaked at one hundred thousand, then dropped off drastically when she returned to Europe.

Unquestionably, the florid signature of Napoleon Sarony at the bottom of a cabinet photograph brought instant recognition both here and abroad during the last quarter of the nineteenth century. Credit for the founding of this specialized branch of photography in America goes handily to Sarony. During his career he collected more than forty thousand negatives of celebrities, gaining American "exclusives" from such stars as Bernhardt and Langtry by paying them royalties. His fame as a theatrical photographer brought literally thousands of ordinary folk to his studio and made him for a while a rich man.

Sarony's personal devotion to photography and his high standards of accomplishment did much to elevate the profession. Certainly his colorful personality did not hinder his advancement. He regarded himself as an artist and he behaved according to the popular conception of the artist, with a display of fascinating eccentricities. Of mixed British, Italian, and French ancestry, Sarony was born in Quebec in 1821, the year that Napoleon Bonaparte died on St. Helena. His given name was rendered even more appropriate in adulthood, when he attained a height of only slightly more than five feet. In 1831 the Sarony family moved to New York City. At the age of ten, Napoleon was apprenticed to a lithographer, and after six years of professional training, some of it with Nathaniel Currier, he founded, with Henry Major, the lithographic firm of Sarony & Major, which, with the addition of a third partner, became Sarony, Major & Knapp. The firm prospered and, having amassed a small fortune, Sarony withdrew from the company and went to Europe to study art and roam. There he was attracted to photography, which was then sweeping the Continent. He opened a studio in Birmingham, England, and at the close of the Civil War, he decided to return to New York. With the proceeds of the sale of his Birmingham business, Sarony opened his first studio, at 630 Broadway, opposite Bond Street, in 1866. Flair coupled with painstaking attention to lighting and posing brought him a large following, particularly among theater people. By 1870 he had moved to larger quarters at 680 Broadway, and a few years later made his final move to 37 Union Square, in the heart of New York's first real theater district.

Partly out of instinct and partly, perhaps, by conscious design, Sarony surrounded his work and studio with an aura of unabashed theatricality. From all reports, going to his spacious Union Square quarters was an experience in itself. A small, slow hydraulic elevator lifted his patrons to his large fifth-floor reception room, where they were greeted at the door by an Egyptian mummy case and a statue of Christopher Columbus. Lining the walls were representations of gods from

Napoleon Sarony, the man who founded the specialty of theatrical photography in the nineteenth century, is shown here in a fake snowstorm contrived through "special effects" in his own studio

Opposite:

In 1865 sex goddess Adah Isaacs Menken visited photographer Napoleon Sarony in his Birmingham, England, studio. She had engaged him to prepare a series of *cartes-de-visite* to publicize her appearance in England in *Mazeppa*. The actress had stipulated that she should choose the poses, and Sarony had agreed—with the proviso that he himself might also arrange her in a series of poses. When the photographs were ready, Menken, of course, preferred the master's set, shown here, to her own

India and China; armor from Japan and England; and guns and pistols from Arabia, Morocco, and Turkey. The rest of the building was crammed with bric-a-brac, antiques, and curios—everything from a human skull to a stuffed crocodile. If he was not able to conjure up the right background for his subjects among his collection, he would retire quickly to his "den" to sketch something appropriate. While his long-time camera operator, Benjamin Richardson, waited patiently, Sarony posed and lighted his subjects, keeping up a running barrage of command, cajolement, and conversation. He draped and arranged and he suffered no interference or suggestion. Since the exposure time could average thirty seconds or more, it was no mean trick to induce his clients to hold a pose while clamped in an iron vise. A very large part of his success as a photographer is attributable to showmanship, an ability to make the "holding" time bearable, even enjoyable. As a writer for *Anthony's Photographic Bulletin* observed in 1884, "He has knowledge of artistic attitude and drapery, and he is such an interesting person."

Sarony left an enormous body of theatrical portraits. All bear his unique stamp, which the caricaturist Thomas Nast, a close friend, attributed to a kind of screening process: "There was one peculiar feature which made his work stand apart from that of anyone else. He made everyone he photographed look like Sarony. You know what I mean. The same feeling was in every picture. Partly from imitation and partly from following out his directions, all his sitters seemed to catch the Sarony tricks of expression and pose. If they did not he would not take them at all."

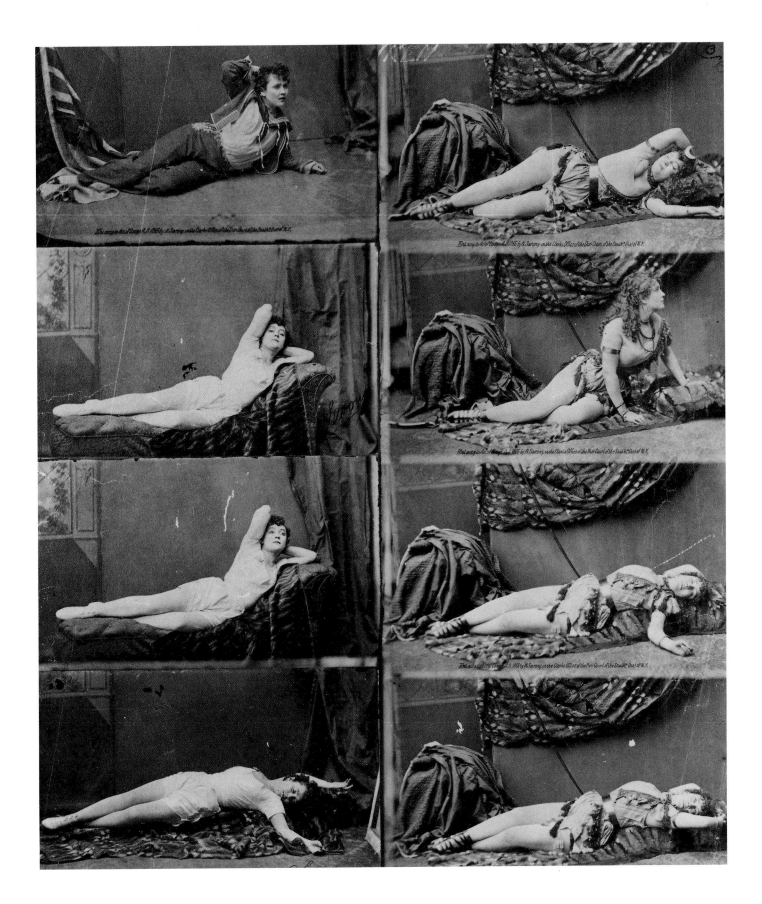

Napoleon Sarony took many pictures of the tragedienne Sarah Bernhardt on her tours in America. All three of these cabinet views were carefully copyrighted in 1880 by the canny photographer, for he paid a considerable sum to a select few of the stars for the exclusive right to photograph them

Opposite:

José Maria Mora, Napoleon Sarony's one-time student and later rival, selected Maud Branscombe (an actress of minimal accomplishments) as his favorite photographic subject. Thousands of photographs of Branscombe in many poses flooded the markets, creating their own vogue, and Mora was able to accumulate a handsome fortune with a minimum of effort. Customers picked the prints they wanted from pages of images on sheets assembled in albums. These pages were the forerunners of the key sheets and contact sheets used by modern photographers for the same purpose

Several years before his death, in 1896, Sarony groomed his son Otto to take over the studio, which was transferred to 256 Fifth Avenue. Otto Sarony continued as a theatrical and celebrity photographer until his own premature death in 1903, and for a number of years thereafter the Sarony name lived on, attached to a chain of photographic studios in Manhattan and Brooklyn.

Napoleon Sarony's success spurred several other photographers in the late nineteenth century into competing for the theater world's custom. José Maria Mora, a Cuban, trained with Sarony before striking out on his own. In 1870 he took over a studio at 707 Broadway, where he appears to have remained for the rest of his active career. He became a serious rival of his former master, attracting hundreds of performers to his door. Mora's trademark was a soft prettiness and he attracted a large female clientele. His streamlined methods of production resulted in the manufacture of hundreds of thousands of photographs, which he called his "publics." They were shipped to all parts of the country and brought him enormous profits. He was last listed as a photographer in business at 707 Broadway in the New York City Directory for 1888–89. Thereafter, he seems to have dropped out of photography and out of sight—perhaps retiring to some South Sea island on the profits of his profession.

After Sarony's death and Mora's disappearance from the New York scene, the photographer who drew most of the theatrical trade was Benjamin J. "Jake" Falk. A native New Yorker and a City College graduate, Falk opened his first studio in 1877 at 347 East Fourteenth Street, not far from the center of the theatrical district at Union Square. Within a few years, he had made his mark and moved to 947–49 Broadway, where he remained for more than a decade. His best-known offices were at 13–15 West Twenty-fourth Street, in the Madison Square area.

Although Falk took better photographs than Sarony and Mora, largely because of improvements in the sensitivity or "speed" of the photographic plate, he courted fame by taking his camera for the first time into a theater to capture the mise-en-scène. For this, Falk had to

Opposite:

Motioning actress Alice Fischer to "hold," Sarony snaps the perfectly arranged figure at his studio. Note the appurtenances of the photographer: neck brace, back support, screen, drapery, and the large camera. To the left of Sarony, another camera was shooting this scene

When Oscar Wilde reached New York in 1882 to begin his famous American lecture tour, one of his first stops was the studio of Napoleon Sarony. This photograph of the characteristically attired esthete against a whimsical yet entirely appropriate backdrop dates from that year. It

was originally printed in the "imperial size," approximately 7 by 10 inches. Sarony's willingness to do battle for his rights led to a legal wrangle that traveled to the Supreme Court. The Burrow-Giles Lithographic Company, which had pirated Sarony's exclusive photographs of Wilde, ar-

gued that their lithographs were different forms of expression, not reproductions. The court disagreed—though not until 1893—and the landmark decision established the photographer as the owner of his prints and the only person who can dispose of the reproduction rights

ELEONORA DUSE.

Pach Bros   935 B'WAY, N.Y.

MAY ROBSON

Opposite:

Dubbed by historian George C. Odell as the "best eccentric comedienne on our stage," May Robson was best known for her "drunk act." This diminutive photograph of the beloved character actress appeared on an advertising card for Sweet Caporal Cigarettes sometime during the late 1890s

The photographic studio with the longest unbroken history of business in New York is Pach Brothers, still in existence today at 16 East Fifty-third Street. Trained by Mathew Brady, Gustavus Pach and his brother Gotthelf founded a studio in New Jersey before moving to New York in 1867. Although the

Pachs' clientele was primarily rooted in the business and political world, the photographers rounded out their list with subjects from the theater. Shown here in a cabinet-size photograph is a pensive Eleonora Duse during one of her tours in America, about the turn of the century

Aimé Dupont worked as a sculptor in Belgium before emigrating to the United States. In 1886 he set up his photographic studio in New York and began to specialize in cabinet photographs of stars of the Metropolitan Opera. Dupont died in 1900, but his studio continued in business under the direction of his wife for several more years. About 1897 Dupont photographed Ada Rehan, star of Augustin Daly's famed theatrical company, in a pose approaching grand-opera magnificence

In April 1887, Elmer Chickering of Boston, that city's leading celebrity photographer, took an ad on the front page of the *Bijou Theatre* (right) to proclaim his status. His charming picture of popular performer Madge Lessing perched on a bicycle (opposite) reveals both the skill of the photographer (he has somehow balanced his subject without the suspicion of a wobble) and the boldness of the actress (she agreed to be shown on the new-fangled and daring invention)

await the development of a dependable and intense artificial light source. Prior to the invention of the incandescent lightbulb, the photographic fraternity relied almost exclusively on sunlight for illumination. Using elaborate skylights and reflectors, first-rank photographers could take portraits in their studios, but their advertisements invariably included the words "on fair days" along with the hours of business. Even the arrival of gaslight in the late nineteenth century did not greatly assist them. It proved too dim, and the flame produced subliminal colors that made it difficult to achieve correct exposures.

On May 1, 1883, with the cooperation of the enlightened management of the Madison Square Theatre, Jake Falk took what he claimed to be the first indoor photograph of a stage scene. The theater manager was Daniel Frohman and the play was an insignificant piece, *The Russian*

A close rival of Napoleon Sarony's was Benjamin "Jake" Falk, who learned photography from George Rockwood. Falk liked to create novel effects and tried to expand the frontiers of his field. In 1883, he moved his camera into the Madison Square Theatre, turned on electric lights strung across the stage, and for the first time in history recorded live theater—giving immortality, unfortunately, to a trivial entertainment entitled *The Russian Honeymoon*. Aware of the significance of the moment, producer Daniel Frohman climbed into costume and took his place onstage and, in the photograph, slightly right of center

Honeymoon, by Mrs. Burton Harrison, a society grande dame with literary aspirations. According to Frohman, Falk strung a crescent of electric lights across the interior of the auditorium and made exposures varying from six to eighteen seconds. The event was duly recorded in newspapers and photographic journals, and the resulting pictures were widely distributed in the cabinet size. Despite attempts by a writer in *Art Amateur,* an early American photographic journal, to refute Falk's claim, and the recent discovery of some amateur efforts dating before 1883, his accomplishment has not been seriously challenged.

Although pictures of stage scenes were immediately recognized for their potential advertising value, Falk's method was too cumbersome for routine use. Exposure time was too long for comfort and, more important, many theaters in the country had not yet converted to electric lighting. With the introduction of flash powder in 1887, photographers were given the means to shorten exposure time and dispense with hot, intense electric lighting.

In 1888 Joseph Byron, an English photographer, moved to New York to set up shop. The grandson of a daguerreotypist and the son of a photographer, he followed family tradition by involving his entire family in the American enterprise. His oldest son, Percy C. Byron, became a full-fledged photographer and member of the firm while still in his teens and took control of the studio upon the death of his father. The Byron Studio had two specialties: photographing the travelers arriving and departing in the passenger ships in New York harbor and chronicling the New York stage. One of Percy's earliest assignments was to take pictures of Edwin Booth's

LILLIAN RUSSELL.

Falk

(OVER.)

949 BROADWAY, N. Y.

LILLIAN RUSSELL.

Falk

(OVER.)

949 BROADWAY, N. Y.

funeral cortege, which he promptly sold to the *New York Herald*. They were reproduced as line drawings in the paper in 1893. It was Joseph Byron who concentrated on stage photography, leaving Percy to meet the boats at Manhattan's docks. When Joseph died, in 1923, the studio's activities in the theater ceased.

The establishment of the Byron studio in New York nearly exactly coincided with the introduction of flash photography in the late nineteenth century. Like many other innovations, flash photography has passed through a long evolution that will probably never end. What it did for Joseph Byron was to make his studio portable and enable him to abandon the time-honored fake backdrops and theatrical gimcrackery in favor of the real thing onstage. To capture the flavor of live dramatic performance, Byron and his assistants would carry their big (11-by-14-inch) camera into a theater, set up a portable platform in the center of the orchestra, scatter two or three technicians around the house with flash charges, and expose as many glass plates as they thought were necessary. By the end of the session, the smoke from the magnesium charges billowed throughout the auditorium and necessitated a thorough airing of the theater. The actors were taxed beyond endurance—something they would not forget when they were ready to face producers at the bargaining table in the years to come.

Joseph Byron sold his scene photographs not only to the illustrated press, sheet-music publishers, and poster printers but to managers and producers. If pictures were taken during the final dress rehearsals, it was possible to have the finished photographs mounted in glass cases

Acting on the national conviction that there could never be too much of "America's Beauty," Benjamin Falk photographed the voluptuous Lillian Russell fore and aft and mounted the views back to back to make a double cabinet photograph

In another inspired moment, Benjamin Falk superimposed the negatives of his photographs of all the actors and actresses of New York's Lyceum Theatre Company and printed two composites. Here are the results

COMPOSITE PORTRAIT
of the Gentlemen of the Lyceum Theatre Company.
949 BROADWAY, N.Y.

COMPOSITE PORTRAIT
of the Ladies of the Lyceum Theatre Company.
949 BROADWAY, N.Y.

outside the theater before the official opening, to pique the curiosity of the casual passersby. The importance of this type of advertisement was not lost upon such canny moguls as Charles Frohman and Henry Savage, who retained the Byron Studio to produce the photography for their shows. Later, Byron and his staff began a tradition of going to the out-of-town tryouts for Broadway shows so that their pictures could be ready for pre–opening-night publicity.

Byron's business blossomed. Since on the average more than a hundred shows opened annually in the first decade of the twentieth century, and since the studio might realize from one hundred to several hundred dollars on each production, the rewards could be considerable. Add to this the pictures made for touring companies—about two hundred fifty a year during this same period. It was no wonder that Byron's success became inspiration to his competitors.

Byron's business stationery bore the words "The Stage Is My Studio," but his actual studio was located for many years at 1260 Broadway. And it was there from 1900 to 1920 that the Byrons made portrait photographs of the performers and celebrities of the New York stage. Sometimes the Byrons were allowed into the homes and apartments of the great stars to catch them in "relaxed moments." Bernhardt admitted the Byrons to her hotel suite so that Joseph could photograph her in an intimate setting. The pictures were later published in the June 1896 edition of *Munsey's Magazine,* pushing the sale of that single issue to seven hundred thousand.

Byron ventured beyond the proscenium arch into the workaday world of the theater and captured rehearsals, stagehands, costumers, actors relaxing in the greenroom, and dressing rooms, stagedoors, producers' offices, scene shops, acting schools—every imaginable aspect of the theater and every type of theater craftsman. He photographed audiences, theater interiors, theater exteriors, proscenium arches, curtains and draperies, and storage areas. Many of these pictures were never published and some were used for manufacturers' brochures, long lost to public view. Whatever impelled him to the task, the end result is a document unparalleled in the history of theatrical iconography. Byron is even more gratefully remembered because, unlike Sarony and his imitators, he never intruded his own personality into his photography. He recognized his role as a recorder and reporter, not an artist or editorializer, and his pictures reveal a kind of interested naiveté. As such, his vision was peerless.

Although New York dominated theatrical photography by virtue of being the wellspring of dramatic activity for the nation at this time, most of the major and many of the minor cities could boast a studio that specialized in theatrical work before 1900. Boston, Chicago, San Francisco, and Philadelphia each had at least one representative. After 1900, with the control of touring companies firmly in the hands of New York businessmen, packets of advertising material containing photographs prepared in New York were routinely sent out ahead of the approaching companies, thus diminishing the importance of the local studio.

Byron's studio had its competitors and imitators, but none achieved its spectacular success. The studio that became heir to the lion's share of theater work in the declining years of the Byron Studio did not in any way resemble the older studio in origin or history. There are any

Large bellows cameras, decorative screens, and even a skylight are visible in this 1898 photograph of Joseph Byron's studio, giving it a superficial resemblance to Napoleon Sarony's old headquarters on Union Square, but Byron worked in the new era of flash photography and chose not to rely so heavily on props. Sarony's stuffed crocodiles and ancient mummy cases have found no place here

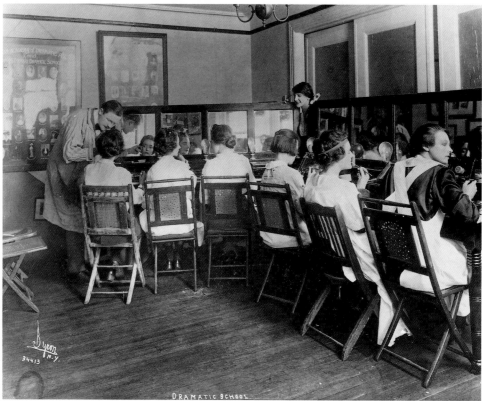

DRAMATIC SCHOOL

Shown are four of the scores of photographs taken offstage and behind the scenes by Joseph Byron and his roving camera. Opposite above: a group of "stage door Johnnies" outside the Empire Theatre, on the southeast corner of Broadway and Fortieth Street; opposite below: a make-up class at the American Academy of Dramatic Arts at its early address on Fifty-seventh Street at Sixth Avenue; above: stage-hands at Wallack's Theatre, just off Union Square; and left: the stage of the Hippodrome Theatre on Sixth Avenue (between Forty-third and Forty-fourth streets) being swept clean by the Vacuum Cleaner Company. All are peerless documents of the theater in New York just before the turn of the century

Many things are revealed in this photograph by Joseph Byron and his staff: the interior configuration of the Bijou Theatre in Brooklyn about the turn of the century; the full house for a performance of that old warhorse *Uncle Tom's Cabin;* and the composition of the audience (mostly female). In that era of primitive flash photography, extraordinary skill and perseverance were needed to produce an indoor group photograph like this

Ethel Barrymore was just twenty-one years old when producer Charles Frohman elevated her to stardom in Clyde Fitch's *Captain Jinks of the Horse Marines* (1901), and a star she remained for the rest of her days. She is shown here in a Joseph Byron photograph of a scene from the first act of the play. (On page 106 is a photograph of the actress taken forty years later)

Early in 1903, the first theatrical adaptation of L. Frank Baum's *Wizard of Oz* opened the new Majestic Theatre on Columbus Circle in New York. It was a triumph for vaudevillians Fred A. Stone as the Scarecrow and Dave Montgomery as the Tin Woodman and for everyone else associated with the show. Joseph Byron photographed this one of many colorful scenes from the production

With herself as star, Mrs. Fiske gained public acceptance of Ibsen's grim, realistic plays through her superb productions and the able support of members of her hand-picked company at the Manhattan Theatre. Using flash photography, Joseph Byron and his staff preserved for posterity this view of the great actress and Claus Bogel onstage in *A Doll's House* in 1902. The setting is representative of the realistic and detailed stage pictures of the era

David Belasco painstakingly directed Mrs. Leslie Carter for her *tour-de-force* performance in *Zaza*, at the Criterion Theatre on Broadway in 1900. No less carefully did Joseph Byron pose Mrs. Carter when he documented this scene in the production. Unfortunately, technology had not yet advanced enough to allow him to capture for posterity her flaming red hair

"THUS DO I DO THE SANTIAGO."
[*Photographed expressly for the "Examiner."*]

In 1893 Carmencita danced between the acts of *The Prodigal Father* at the California Theatre in San Francisco. The *Examiner* sent its photographer to take pictures, which were converted at the newspaper into a series of line drawings and published as such. Only four years later, the photographs themselves could have been reproduced in the newspaper through a process by which images are transformed into constellations of dots on the printing plate, a technique known as halftone photoengraving

Byron's success inspired many imitators. One of the films that siphoned off some of Byron's theatrical business was Hall's Studio at 1456 Broadway. The scene shown is from *In Dahomey*, which made theatrical history in 1903 as the first full-length musical written and played by blacks in a major Broadway theater. Three of the principals are shown: George Walker (left), Ada Overton Walker (center), and Bert Williams (right)

number of stories about how and why the White Studio got into the business, all of them interesting but none verifiable. According to Ralph Shacklee, one of Luther White's chief photographers, White never took a photograph in his life. Luther was in fact a Bowery saloon keeper. Shacklee's version of the founding of the White Studio begins with a saloon customer, a photographer by profession, who ran up a considerable bill at the bar. White devised a way for him to work off his debt by setting up a studio behind the saloon. At that very moment, the city council had just passed an ordinance compelling all Chinese males to cut off their traditional pigtails. To prove that they had done so, they were required to produce a photograph in profile. Since White's backyard studio was a step from the heart of Chinatown, his business boomed, allowing him to abandon the saloon in favor of the photographic studio.

Hope White, Luther's granddaughter, offered another version of the tale. According to her, White bought a photographic studio, then persuaded his friends in Tammany Hall to get the discriminatory ordinance passed. Fascinating as these versions are, there is no evidence that a pigtail law was ever passed in New York City. It may be, however, that upon arriving in New York Chinese males quickly divested themselves of the hirsute symbols of their former servility in imperial China and had pictures taken of themselves to send home to friends and relatives to prove their emancipation. Whatever the origin of the studio, Luther White waxed prosperous and was able to move his studio to Fourteenth Street and Third Avenue and to branch out into other kinds of photography. His venture into theatrical photography began with the shooting of *The Virginian,* a big hit of 1904 at the Manhattan Theatre. Within a few years, White's began keeping

Said to have been the first Broadway show photographed by the White Studio, *The Virginian* (1904) starred Dustin Farnum, who was later to go to Hollywood and almost single-handedly launch the era of the film cowboy. Farnum is seen here in a magazine reproduction of one of the White Studio photographs, with his costar, Gretchen Lyons

Rain, a play that opened in 1922 and quickly gained nationwide notoriety, starred Jeanne Eagels as the unregenerate prostitute Sadie Thompson, the role of her career. Unfortunately, the White Studio photographs and proofs for this and other plays were printed on inferior grades of photographic paper, and many examples now reposing in theater collections throughout the country are in poor condition and in desperate need of preservation. This print, showing (left to right) Harold Healy, Kent Thurber, Harry Quealy, Eagels, Robert Elliott, and Rapley Holmes, is an example of how harshly time has dealt with the White Studio legacy

"keysheets," pages of reduced prints similar to today's contact sheets, from which the producer or the stars could make a selection. These keysheets, maintained from 1910 to 1936, represent the most comprehensive record of the American stage during that time, since at its height, White's photographed nearly 85 percent of all productions originating in New York and most going on the road.

The theatrical specialty did so well that White's moved again, in the late 1910s, to the Candler Building at 220 West Forty-second Street, in the heart of the new theater district abuilding around Times Square. Shacklee did the portrait work in the studio, while a Canadian photographer, George Lucas, went out into the field to take the stage shots. Lucas and White are credited with improving Byron's cumbersome method of flash photography by introducing smokeless flash powder that could be ignited instantly by air blown through a hose.

The White Studio photographs never quite matched Byron's in quality and care. Lacking Joseph Byron's singleness of vision, White's staff of photographers produced work that varies

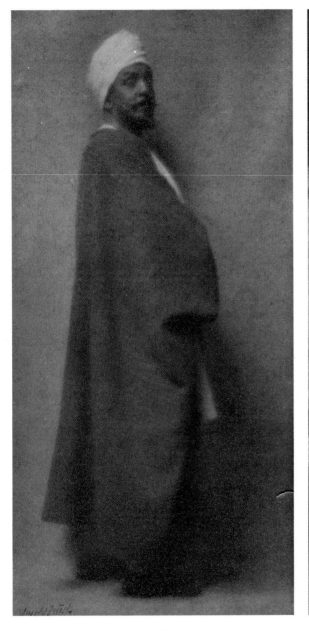

The young Berlin-born scholar and philologist Arnold Genthe opened a photographic studio in San Francisco in 1899 (there he chronicled the great earthquake of 1906). Primarily a portrait photographer, Genthe journeyed to New York in 1911 to continue his career. Soft focus and selective retouching give a dreamy quality to his subjects. This photograph of Otis Skinner in *Kismet* (1911) is revealing of Genthe's idiosyncratic technique, which he applied to his favorite subject, Isadora Duncan, and to his many celebrity clients

The great impresario Florenz Ziegfeld was more than just a discoverer of stage talent. He appears to have had a sensitive eye for photography. When he saw the amateur efforts of a young art student named Alfred Cheney Johnston, he persuaded him to give up his studies and become the official photographer of the Ziegfeld Follies in 1918. Johnston went on to photograph all the great beauties under Ziegfeld's management, none of whom was more famous than Marilyn Miller, who is shown here, about 1920, in her typical toe-dancing pose, all fluffy tutu and golden curls

Specializing in onstage work, the White Studio did not venture frequently into portrait photography, but occasionally the White photographers produced an outstanding example of the genre. Shown here is the English actress Cathleen Nesbitt, who came to New York in 1916 to star in a repertory of plays. Her career spanned nearly eight decades on both the English and the American stages; she is probably best remembered here as Rex Harrison's mother in *My Fair Lady*. In this lovely and rare photograph she is probably in costume for *Great Catherine* (1916)

from show to show. Much of it looks rushed and suffers from flatness and lifelessness, and because they were printed on inferior paper many of the prints have disintegrated. Nor does White's portrait work compare with that of Arnold Genthe, Nickolas Muray, G. M. Kesselere or Alfred Cheney Johnston—all of whom were contributing celebrity portraits to the leading magazines of the time. The preeminence of the White Studio may be attributable in part to an association with Lee and J. J. Shubert, for whom the studio became the "house" photographer. The Shuberts dominated theatrical production during the 1920s and provided more than enough work for the studio. But if the Shuberts were responsible for White's financial success, they also contributed to its failure. After the crash of 1929, the Shuberts defaulted on their debts to White, as did Florenz Ziegfeld and other bankrupt producers, and the studio faltered badly. Out of loyalty, White allowed his association with the Shuberts to continue longer than was healthy for the studio, and he suffered additional losses.

Luther White died in 1936, his son three years later. Their studio was disbanded and regrouped by George Lucas and Irving Pritchard, White's business manager. Later, Edward Thayer Monroe, an established Broadway and portrait photographer, joined the studio, which during the 1930s became known as the Lucas and Monroe Studio. It was finally overwhelmed by a formidable woman named Florence Vandamm, whose studio very nearly created a monopoly on theatrical photography for thirty years.

Almost from the dawn of the photographic age, women entered the field on almost equal footing with men. Perhaps the explanation lies in the fact that they are not obliged to venture far afield, since the studio and darkroom can be set up under the home roof to become a kind of cottage industry. Women brought to photography their own vision and were free to make their contributions without the usual struggles they encountered in practically every other vocation. Florence Van Damm (later shortened to Vandamm) was born in London in 1883, the daughter of a solicitor. After studying art, she became a professional miniaturist, opening her own studio in 1908. Recognizing that photography could be of help to her as a portraitist, she studied photographic and darkroom techniques at the London Polytechnic and eventually abandoned painting in favor of photography. In 1918 she married George Robert Thomas, an American, to whom she taught photography. Together they founded a studio that became so successful that they were able to move to stylish Bond Street. They added fashion photography to their portrait work and contributed regularly to the American magazines *Vogue* and *Vanity Fair*.

In 1937, the White Studio (reorganized and renamed Lucas-Pritchard) photographed Max Reinhardt's production *The Eternal Road.* This biblical spectacle by Franz Werfel with music by Kurt Weill employed well nigh the entire theatrical community. Staged at the Manhattan Opera House, the show was designed by Norman Bel Geddes. Nearly one hundred cast members are onstage in this photograph

Association with the theater world was inevitable for Nickolas Muray (1892–1965), since his first portrait studio was on Mac-Dougal Street in New York, not far from the Provincetown Playhouse, which was, during the 1920s, the most successful of the experimental little theaters. It was just a question of time before Muray would photograph the most important member of the group, Eugene O'Neill, and this fine three-quarters profile of the playwright was published in *Theatre Magazine* in December 1922. Muray went on to work for *Vanity Fair* and produced many portraits of the rich, famous, and celebrated.

When their clientele fell off after the war, they decided to try their luck in New York, settling into an apartment-*cum*-studio at Fiftieth Street and Sixth Avenue, where now stands Radio City Music Hall. Their first real break came in 1928, when they were offered a contract to photograph all of the Theatre Guild's productions. The excellence of their work led to other contracts, and eventually they were photographing about three-quarters of all the productions that reached Broadway. Florence was responsible for the portrait work, while "Tommy" went out into the field to do the stage shots, although he frequently ventured into portrait photography as well. (In a reversal of custom, it was he who assumed his wife's name, rechristening himself Tommy Vandamm.)

Because they were trying to break new ground, the Theatre Guild hired the experimental photographer Francis Bruguière to chronicle their productions on film. He remained with them until 1928, when he left New York for London. Bruguière was never content to produce merely faithful images but sought to capture the psychology of what he saw through the lens. He often altered stage lighting so that he could find some shape or form that would define a play. In this 1920 study of Eugene O'Neill's *The Emperor Jones,* he reduced the setting to a doorway and a throne and placed actors Jasper Deeter and Charles S. Gilpin in a shaft of light

In the flush of their success, they moved to 130 West Fifty-seventh Street, once the home of the American Impressionist painter Childe Hassam. They developed a shrewd critical and business judgment about their work. They cultivated press agents, who had become by then a permanent part of the Broadway theatrical scene, and avoided the shoestring producer. Tommy Vandamm would preview the shows he was assigned to photograph in out-of-town tryouts, traveling with two assistants and six cases of equipment. John Chapman, the daily theater reviewer for the *New York Daily News,* paid tribute to the uncanny accuracy of his assessment of the box-office potential of the plays coming to Broadway. Tommy saw each production through at least once, and sometimes twice, before photographing it, making notes along the way.

This early Vandamm photograph, probably taken at the studio in 1927, shows the young Barbara Stanwyck with old-timer Hal Skelly, beloved of New York audiences. The two were appearing in *Burlesque,* a production that launched Miss Stanwyck's career and sent her off to Hollywood

Opposite:

During his long life (1879–1973), Edward Steichen progressed from work as a lithographer to his true calling as a photographer. A disciple of Alfred Stieglitz, he was one of the earliest photographers to make out of a process an art. His portraiture, appearing mainly in *Vanity Fair,* was famous for its soft focus and lighting. This renowned portrait made in 1922 of British actor and playwright Noel Coward catches the sophistication and brittleness of its subject

STEICHEN, Edward. Noel Coward. (1932) Gelatine-silver print, 16 9/16 by 13 5/16 inches. Collection, The Museum of Modern Art, New York. Gift of the photographer

Recognizing that time meant money to the producers who were paying the cast and crew in overtime, he prepared for the sessions by always knowing what moments he wanted to shoot. He used the precious photo-call time to pose the actors while his assistants adjusted the equipment. In an article on his technique for *Theatre Arts,* he said that he always welcomed suggestions from the company before a session began. He preferred the composed "still" to the candid shot except in the case of dance photography, in which a sense of movement was all-important. He always retouched the photographs he took, explaining that he was returning to the actors' faces the character and personality that stage makeup removed.

Many of Florence's subjects went to her studio directly from the theater, arriving still in costume at all times of the day and night. There, away from the hectic theater milieu, she could take her time to capture not only the well-known faces of the players but also something of the personalities of the characters they were portraying. Vandamm was one of the first women to be elected a member of the Royal Photographic Society, an honor she prized above all others. In 1944 Tommy Vandamm died, at the age of fifty-seven. Florence continued the business, working both in the studio and in the field until 1955, when she retreated to the studio for the rest of her active career. On her retirement, in 1961, she closed down the Vandamm Studio and sold her negatives and prints to the New York Public Library.

The Vandamms' photographic opus is a peerless testament to carefully planned lighting and laborious method. Vandamm photographs are beautiful but never appear spontaneous. Faces are set off to best advantage; no one looks ugly or awkward; the artificiality of the backgrounds is never apparent; and each "still" is balanced and satisfying to the eye. Since theirs was a carefully manicured vision, there is an icy ethereality about their work, a remoteness that probably

Ben Pinchot was a celebrity portraitist who regularly photographed the stars and other theatrical personalities. All portrait photographers learn to use light and shadow to reveal character, but Pinchot's work verges on the painterly. This textural quality is evident in his moody portrait of Maria Ouspenskaya in the 1936 production of *The Daughters of Atreus*. Ouspenskaya, a member of Stanislavsky's Moscow Art Theatre, chose to remain in America when the troupe had completed its American tour. She became renowned both as an actress and as a teacher

Marcus Blechman, portrait photographer of dance and theater personalities from the mid-1930s to the mid-1950s, used a combination of mood music and alcoholic beverage to induce his subjects (mainly women) to strike the right poses. He was a master of lighting and the retouching pencil, and with them he made his subjects seemingly glow. Blechman was reputedly Tallulah Bankhead's photographer of choice, and she is seen here in one of his portraits from the 1940s

When in 1928 Florence and Tommy Vandamm signed a contract to photograph all of the Theatre Guild productions, little did they know that they would be capturing the most important plays, players, and performances to appear on the American stage during the twentieth century. Since the Guild was Eugene O'Neill's producer, the Vandamm Studio photographed all of his major works, from *Dynamo* (1929) to *The Iceman Cometh* (1946). Shown in these two Vandamm photographs are the stars in both productions: Claudette Colbert and Glenn Anders in *Dynamo* (left) and James Barton in *The Iceman Cometh* (below)

Said to have been one of Tommy Vandamm's favorite portraits, this photograph of Lynn Fontanne as the regal protagonist of *Elizabeth the Queen* (1930) took three-quarters of an hour to shoot because of the special lighting effects Vandamm wanted to achieve. In 1937 the photograph was used in an exhibition at the Museum of the City of New York of the Vandamm Studio's work

constituted the quintessence of theatricality in their era. Like the Byron Studio's oeuvre, the Vandamm collection makes wonderful history. Altogether, it represents a document of inestimable value, although future generations must be aware that what they are seeing in the photographs was filtered through a very special eye, and for a balanced view they must study the photographs by other professionals of the era.

Though the Vandamms clung to the stationary 8-by-10 inch camera and continued to rely heavily on retouching, they were undoubtedly abreast of the developments in cameras, film, and photographic accessories that were being made both before and during World War II. The light meter had been developed in the early 1930s; film speed (or sensitivity to light) was

Katharine Cornell, her star constantly ascendant during the 1930s, appeared on Broadway almost every season in a hit play. Among her important productions of the decade was George Bernard Shaw's *Candida* (1937), in which she scored a critical triumph. The many Vandamm photographs of Cornell as Candida had wide circulation. At left is Cornell in the original production. Above she is shown in one of the many revivals of her great starring vehicle

John Gielgud and Lillian Gish, stars of the brilliant 1936 production of *Hamlet* on Broadway, sat for these magnificent photographs by the Vandamm Studio. Portraits of the stars, usually the province of Florence Vandamm, were always taken under carefully arranged conditions

improving rapidly; and smaller, hand-held cameras, producing first 2¼-by-2¼-inch negatives and then 35-millimeter negatives, quickly gained favor with the photographic corps, who were ever eager to divest themselves of cases of heavy gear. The small camera with its rapid film produced immediate, spontaneous "candid" pictures that could be quickly developed, broken up into thousands of tiny dots, and eventually, sent by wire to a printing press thousands of miles away.

One of the first of the new wave of theatrical photographers was Eileen Darby. Growing up in Portland, Oregon, in the late 1920s, she was interested in photography by her father, a skilled amateur, who taught her darkroom techniques; later, as an amateur herself, she took pictures of the Ballet Russe de Monte Carlo on tour in Portland. In 1937 she went to New York and worked with the great Alfred Eisenstaedt. Eventually, she was hired as an assignment photographer for Graphic House, a professional photo agency, and she began taking pictures of Broadway shows. Her theatrical pictures began to turn up regularly in *Life, Time,* and *Newsweek,* and she began to get assignments from the leading press agents. One of them, the late Bernard Simon, remembered seeing her with a camera slung around her neck clambering over seats during the regular photo calls to shoot her pictures. (The official photo call, according to union contract, allowed three hours for a play and four for a musical.) Like Tommy Vandamm, she would frequently travel to out-of-town tryouts to photograph final dress rehearsals. Her career as a theatrical photographer lasted approximately twenty-five years, from 1940 to 1965. Retired now, she admits that her interest in and enthusiasm for the theater ended at about the time the revolutionary 1960s rock musical *Hair* reached Broadway.

Darby's work marked the beginning of a new era in theatrical photography. She recorded more shows than any other photographer of her time and had a profound influence upon the profession, which has persisted to this day. The polished-marble look of Vandamm photographs gave way to more loosely composed, grainier, less self-conscious pictures—all the result of different techniques, better lighting, newer equipment, and union-imposed time restrictions.

At any given moment in history, the financial success of a theatrical photographic studio depends heavily on the health and stability of Broadway. During the early decades of the twentieth century, theater blossomed into a nationwide industry and profit was the byword. When producers were making money, the theatrical photographer flourished. Tommy Vandamm took eleven thousand photographs of the 1939 Lindsay and Crouse hit, *Life with Father,* duly chronicling every cast change and every newsworthy or noteworthy event and every anniversary of its seemingly endless career. If a show was a failure, or if, having deliberated carefully, the producer considered his latest production a chancy venture, no photo call was issued and the play quietly slipped into oblivion. The actors in a shoestring production might be sent to the photographer's studio, where the sets and action would be simulated to look as if they were taken onstage. From the Byron era onward, most of the photographers who specialized in theatrical work also took on nontheatrical assignments to keep bread on the table.

Although the Vandamms went into the theaters to photograph the stars in action, occasionally, and usually because a producer was economizing, the stars came in costume to the famous studio on Fifty-seventh Street. This carefully posed study from *Of Mice and Men* (1937), sans a scenic background, was apparently not taken in the theater. Shown are Broderick Crawford, Wallace Ford, and Claire Luce (left to right), the principals of the production

The young star of Rodgers and Hart's *Pal Joey* (1940), Gene Kelly, later transferred his talents to Hollywood and rose to the heights of movie fame, but hardly anyone remembers that the ingenue of the musical was Leila Ernst. The actors are shown together in this handsome Vandamm photograph

Opposite:

During the 1930s, no play more clearly bespoke the coming of age of the American theater than Thornton Wilder's *Our Town*, which opened in New York at Henry Miller's Theatre in 1938. The young lovers were portrayed by John Craven and Martha Scott. They are seen here on that unforgettable bare stage against which the play was performed. Photograph by the Vandamm Studio

After the Vandamms and Eileen Darby, the careers of theatrical photographers grew shorter and more precarious. The studio that fell heir to the specialty after Darby's retreat from the field was Friedman-Abeles, which flourished roughly from the mid-1950s to the 1970s. The three partners in the enterprise, Joseph Abeles, Leo Friedman, and Sy Friedman (the two Friedmans were not related), divided the work among themselves and dominated the specialty until they, too, gave up the field to vigorous competition.

The reigning theatrical photographer today is Martha Swope, who hails from Waco, Texas. She migrated to New York in the mid-1950s to study dance. As a hobby, she began taking pictures of her classmates and teachers and sold prints on an informal basis to anyone who

Ruth McKenney's stories about her sister first appeared in the *New Yorker*, but the heroine achieved true immortality on the stage. In 1940 *My Sister Eileen* became a vastly successful play and in 1953 a hit musical *(Wonderful Town)*. The studio of Lucas and Monroe caught this scene from the play, which starred Shirley Booth as Ruth and Jo Ann Sayers as the irresistible Eileen

wanted them. In 1957 Jerome Robbins asked her to photograph rehearsals of *West Side Story*, which he was currently staging on Broadway. *Life* accepted one of the pictures for publication and set her on a different course. Once launched in her new career, she began a long period of self-education in camera technique.

For many years, she has linked herself to the dance world, becoming the official photographer for the New York City Ballet and American Ballet Theatre, and for Martha Graham. Her pictures landed on the covers of *Time* and *Newsweek* as well as magazines of smaller circulation, and she published books of dance photographs. In 1963 she tried her hand again at theatrical photography, shooting the first season of the Repertory Theatre of Lincoln Center in their temporary Greenwich Village quarters. She soon found her freelance work being snapped up by press agents, who were impressed by its combination of fidelity to the subject (always of prime importance to this no-nonsense corps) and its liveliness. Her pictures always contained more than an array of actors against an artificial background. Because they conveyed a sense of movement on the stage, they could capture the curiosity of the public. David Merrick, Harold Prince, Mike Nichols, and Neil Simon asked their press agents to hire her, and Swope inevitably became Broadway's unofficial photographic chronicler. Today her studio shoots about 80 percent of all the Broadway productions. Like her predecessors, she packs up her cameras and she and her assistants travel throughout the country to catch pre-Broadway tryouts or rehearsals. She laments that she often has woefully little time to shoot all that she must during the photo calls. Such other encumbrances as the stars' right

Never hesitant about catching actors with their eyes closed, their mouths open, or their bodies akimbo, Eileen Darby used stop-action—"candid"—photography to give an immediacy and freshness to her photographs of Broadway, most of which she took on a freelance basis and sold to *Life* and the daily newspapers, as well as to the press agents for the show. Here are two of Darby's cast photographs from the 1940s: *Carousel* (1945) (left) and *Allegro* (1947) (below)

Because of its longevity (3,224 performances on Broadway), photographing *Life with Father* (1939) became almost a full-time career for Tommy Vandamm. He made a practice of posing the main characters, Mother and Father Day, in each of the cast changes. Shown across this page and the next, in chronological order, from the original actors to the final pair, are Dorothy Stickney and How-ard Lindsay; Margalo Gillmore and Percy Waram; Dorothy Gish and Louis Calhern; Dorothy Gish and Stanley Ridges; Lily Cahill and Wallis Clark; Nydia Westman and Arthur Margetson; Harry Bannister and Muriel Kirkland; Mary Loane and Brandon Peters

to approve pictures, the less than ideal conditions under which she must work, and the relentless rush that pervades her assignments make it difficult for her to edit her work thoughtfully and preserve it for posterity. She is also very conscious that the vogue for theatrical photographers appears to be generational—a thought that she dislikes pursuing.

Swope uses traditional set-ups with extra or special lights (strobes and flood lamps to augment the stage lighting), but she always shoots with a candid camera as well. She is likely to work with both color and black-and-white film at the same time. She brings to her photography the vitality that is the striking feature of her personality, plus unswerving dedication to a world she unabashedly loves. Like her colleagues past and current, she recognizes that success depends upon being available at all times and being able to accomplish assignments rapidly. With the demands upon her heavy and the rewards light, she persists in a specialty in which the world she photographs becomes smaller each year.

The lot of the Broadway theatrical photographer has become ever more precarious, but making a living shooting Off Broadway productions was from the beginning well-nigh impossible. In the flush days of Off Broadway, during the late 1950s and the early 1960s, there were perhaps a half-dozen photographers covering the booming anticommercial and anti-establishment theater—and perhaps one or two of them were making enough to cover the time spent and materials purchased. By its very nature, Off Broadway was an impecunious theater and prided itself on its ability to provide rousing or riveting entertainment without the trappings of commercialism. If there was anything left over—and there usually was not—it might go to pay a photographer for a record of the production.

Only two photographers were to last the course and both went to New York from Chicago. Alix Jeffry arrived in 1952, and during the next sixteen years she accumulated forty thousand photographs and negatives of two hundred fifty seminal and original productions, debuts of performers on their way to stardom, playwrights on the verge of recognition, fledgling dance companies, and world premieres of avant-garde plays. She frequently took photographs of shows from rehearsal to opening night and beyond, establishing a complete record of the genesis of the

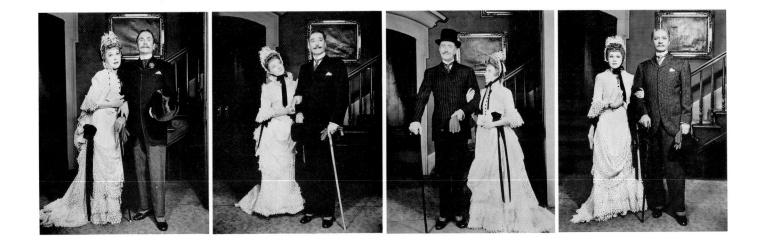

The photograph taken in the heat of the action onstage was Eileen Darby's specialty, but the technique was taken up by a host of competitors, both independent photographers and studios. The most important studio after Vandamm's was Friedman-Abeles, which received such major assignments as *My Fair Lady*, the triumphant musical hit of 1956. Because of the elegance of the costumes and settings, it was also one of the most photographed productions of all time. Shown here is the tea party in *My Fair Lady* (left to right: Cathleen Nesbitt, Julie Andrews, John Michael King)

In 1959 *A Raisin in the Sun* catapulted the black playwright Lorraine Hansberry and the cast to clear and deserved fame. By choosing a "frozen-motion" pose reminiscent of the Vandamm Studio style, Friedman-Abeles was able to concentrate attention on Claudia McNeil's wonderfully expressive face during a moving moment in the play

Still reflecting the carefully posed and perfectly balanced style of Vandamm Studio photographs is this picture of a scene from *The King and I,* starring Gertrude Lawrence, in 1951, long after the death in 1944 of Tommy Vandamm

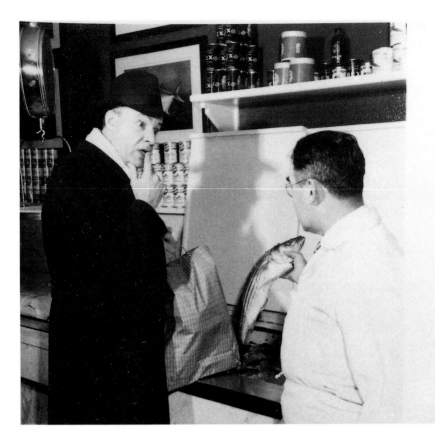

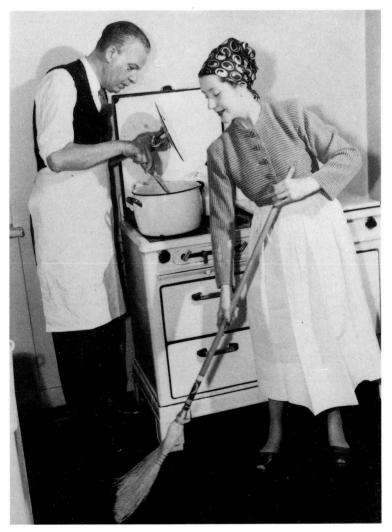

The late Broadway publicist Bernard Simon referred to the group of freelance photographers armed with small cameras who regularly attended photo sessions for shows as "bathroom photographers" because, in his words, "they didn't have a proper darkroom, but developed and printed in their home bathrooms." At the top of this list he placed Bob Golby, who photographed the New York theater and its celebrities from 1935 to 1972. In these candid shots, taken in 1946, Golby caught the Lunts (Alfred Lunt and Lynn Fontanne) performing the humblest of offstage business right in their own home and at their local market

Another early outstanding free-lance photographer was Fred Fehl, a refugee from Nazi Austria, who turned his hobby into a profession when he arrived in America in 1939. In the following year Fehl appeared at a theatrical photo call with his 35-millimeter Leica and began shooting pictures using only the available stage light. When he was able to sell the results, his fate was sealed and he embarked on a career as a freelance theatrical and dance photographer that was to last nearly thirty years. Shown here is a dance scene from the musical *Fiorello!* (1959). Note that Fehl's frame catches the orchestra pit as well as the stage in order to make it clear that this is an unposed, un-rehearsed stage-performance photograph

During its long history, *Life* magazine gave employment to just about every outstanding photographer in America. At one time or another, all of them were assigned to cover the New York theater, and such names as Cecil Beaton, Cornell Capa, Alfred Eisenstaedt, Eliot Elisofon, George Karger, Philippe Halsman, Edward Steichen, John Swope, and Ralph Morse appeared below the photographs. Few captured on-stage action better than Gjon Mili, who used the stroboscope ("strobe"), an instrument that emits a powerful, brilliant, but brief light in synchronization with sensitive film to produce photographs that seem to spring to life as one gazes at them. Here pictured is a poignant moment from the 1957 production of Eugene O'Neill's *A Moon for the Misbegotten*, with principals (left to right) Wendy Hiller, William Woodson, and Cyril Cusack

Familiar with her work as an amateur dance photographer, director-choreographer Jerome Robbins asked Martha Swope to photograph his production of *West Side Story* (1960). Swope subsequently abandoned her dance career for the precarious life of a theatrical photographer. In this vivid shot, the male dancers, representing one of the rival street gangs of New York's West Side, are poised for action

Using a hand-held camera, Martha Swope consumes roll after roll of film as she strives to catch the electricity onstage in at least some of her shots. Rather than setting up what she wants to record, Swope relies on her quick response to the action onstage to reveal the essence of the play or musical. Here captured is a moment of hilarity in *Company*, the Stephen Sondheim musical of 1970, with (left to right) George Coe, Teri Ralston, and Dean Jones

Frank Langella as Count Dracula in the 1977 revival of Bram Stoker's mystery thriller looks appropriately menacing framed against an Edward Gorey setting in this Martha Swope photograph

The slender and lanky six-foot-six-inch frame of performer-director-choreographer Tommy Tune becomes a part of the pipes, lines, and pulleys of backstage in this 1980 photographic study by Martha Swope

Since 1974 Gerry Goodstein has made a career photographing Off Broadway shows and regional theater productions. His earliest ambition was to be an actor, but after study at the New York Institute of Photography he switched his sights and got his first jobs as a commercial photographer. After more than two years working in Martha Swope's studio, Goodstein branched out on his own. He is now the photographic chronicler of such New York theatrical groups as Playwrights Horizons, Circle Repertory Theatre, and the Manhattan Theatre Club, and he has also ranged the East Coast, from Massachusetts to Florida, photographing major regional theaters. Here shown is a Goodstein photograph from the 1987 Manhattan Theatre Club production of *Hunting Cockroaches*, a play by Polish dramatist Janusz Glowacki. It starred Dianne Wiest and Ron Silver

The bravura acting of Jessica Tandy and Hume Cronyn seen here in *The Gin Game* (1977), could never have been adequately recorded on film, but Martha Swope's revealing picture of these two consummate actors deep in the intricacies of performance represents the best that can be done with still photography in preserving theatrical moments on film

Historians must give due credit to photographer Alix Jeffry for preserving important moments in the theater through her careful chronicling of the Off Broadway movement in New York. Relying solely on ambient light, she was able to capture for the ages the transient experience of live performance—as in this photograph taken in 1955 of Judith Malina surrounded by members of the Living Theatre in a production of Luigi Pirandello's *Tonight We Improvise*

play and production. Tracking the career of Edward Albee from downtown to uptown, she covered his Broadway production of *Tiny Alice* beginning in 1962 with photographs of the stars, John Gielgud and Irene Worth, as they arrived by plane for rehearsals in New York and ending with the opening-night party at the producer's home. Her photographs were featured in major publications throughout the country and still appear from time to time in histories of the period. Her entire work now resides at the Harvard Theatre Collection, an archive in Cambridge, Massachusetts, that any serious student of Off Broadway theater must consult.

The other Chicagoan, Bert Andrews, arrived with his family at the age of six and was educated in New York's schools and colleges before an opportunity to learn the techniques of photography during military service in Germany turned his interests in that direction. Always fascinated by the theater, he began his career as a theatrical photographer by shooting a production of *Dark of the Moon,* directed by Vinnette Carroll at the Harlem YMCA in 1960. (In the cast were Cicely Tyson, James Earl Jones, Roscoe Lee Browne, and Clarence Williams III.) He was paid ten dollars for the job, plus ninety cents a print. For three years Andrews photographed the productions of the Equity Library Theatre in Manhattan, but his first major break was as production photographer of *The Blacks* in 1961. He has since photographed all of the productions of the Negro Ensemble Company but one. A disastrous fire in his studio apartment in 1985 consumed more than one thousand negatives and prints. Fortunately, four exhibitions of his prints were traveling around the metropolitan area at the time and are preserved, and the Schomberg Center for Research in Black Culture, to which he had willed his collection, possesses others, as do several other libraries and museums in the New York area. Recognizing the historical value of his work, he and his friends have been trying to reconstruct his collection from prints of all of the Off Broadway productions he has shot during his career.

Although photography represents the single most important record and proof of performance that we have, it is probably the most slighted by commercial and non-profit theaters today. When it cannot be used for promoting a show, it is considered a frill by the producers. Happily, most important regional theaters throughout the country employ a photographer to shoot each production as a record of their accomplishments.

Beginning a little more than one hundred years ago with an eccentric little photographer in a quirky Union Square studio, theatrical photography has never made millionaires of its practitioners, but it has enriched the history of the theater as no other kind of documentation could. It has provided us with tantalizing clues as to how theatrical productions were mounted in bygone decades, how players looked and acted, and how photography itself played a role in publicizing shows, improving the quality of show paper, and generally enlivening the theatrical experience for an eager audience.

BETWEEN THE ACTS & BRAVO
CIGARETTES

E. A. SOTHERN.

LITH. OF HEPPENHEIMER & MAURER, 22 & 24 N. WM ST N.Y.

BETWEEN THE ACTS & BRAVO
CIGARETTES

MINNIE HAUK.

LITH. OF HEPPENHEIMER & MAURER, 22 & 24 N. WM ST N.Y.

N. C. Goodwin
IN THE HUNCHBACK

Lotta

ALLEN & GINTER'S
CIGARETTES
RICHMOND, VIRGINIA.

MARIE BURROUGHS.

Celebrity in the late nineteenth century meant having your picture appear on an advertising card for cigarettes or candy or soap. Usually inserted in the wrappings of the product, the tiny portraits were as avidly collected as are baseball cards today. Here shown are a few specimens bearing the likenesses of performers famous in their time

Arrived in America from his native Italy in 1927, Alfredo Valente tried at first to support himself as a painter, but circumstances led him eventually to photography. For four years (1934–38), he worked as staff photographer for *Stage* magazine while also serving as the official chronicler of Group Theatre productions (1933–41). His colleagues and competitors the Vandamms were never happy working with color film, but Valente realized that color photography was coming of age and that publishers of newspapers and magazines were becoming more receptive to its use. His stage photographs in color are among the earliest that can be found in theatrical archives. Here shown are three Valente portrait photographs of the grandes dames of the theater in the late 1930s and early 1940s. Upper left: Beatrice Lillie when she was appearing in *Set to Music* (1939); upper right: Ethel Barrymore in *The Corn is Green* (1940); right: Katharine Hepburn in *Without Love* (1942)

During the 1950s, four-color printing flowed freely for the first time through programs, newspapers, and magazines, and producers and press agents flocked to the Friedman-Abeles Studio for color photographs of current shows—like this one from the 1959 hit *The Sound of Music*, starring Mary Martin

Martha Swope regularly photographs with both color and black-and-white film, since color is now routinely splashed through most magazines and becomes increasingly common in newspapers. She remains the official chronicler of the New York Public Theater and its Shakespeare Festival and is currently photographing Joseph Papp's productions of the Bard's entire canon for the Public Theater. She was on hand to capture the 1988 summer production of Shakespeare's *Much Ado about Nothing*, with Kevin Kline and Blythe Danner, seen here in lively disputation

Magazines

In 1927, as the theatrical bubble was rising higher and higher, manager Arthur Hammerstein built a theater on Broadway in honor of his legendary father, Oscar, and placed in a copper box in the cornerstone of the playhouse his father's silk top hat, a cigar (Oscar's signature)—and a copy of *Theatre Magazine*, then the reigning popular show-business monthly. Splashy, colorful theatrical magazines like *Theatre* have all but disappeared from their customary place on the living-room coffee table, but in the boom years of the theater in America—when the stage show was the only dramatic entertainment available—everyone wanted to keep up with the latest events in the lives of the stars and to read about what was happening on Broadway. Today, all that remains of this staple of family reading are a few specialized or scholarly magazines or journals that reach a limited public nationally. Collected chiefly by libraries, they may be sought out in their quiet precincts.

In the English-speaking world, serials or periodicals (library terms for magazines) have been around for almost three hundred years and were the offspring of newspapers, which have been around even longer. Today, newspapers and magazines print much the same kind of material, but for the sake of definition we say that newspapers deal mainly with events as they happen and magazines mainly review events some time after they have happened. In theory, the writing in magazines should be better and more thoughtful. Perhaps that explains their higher cost.

The English writer Daniel Defoe is given credit for creating the first magazine, but he owed something to Montaigne and Bacon for their efforts in perfecting the essay and to the French

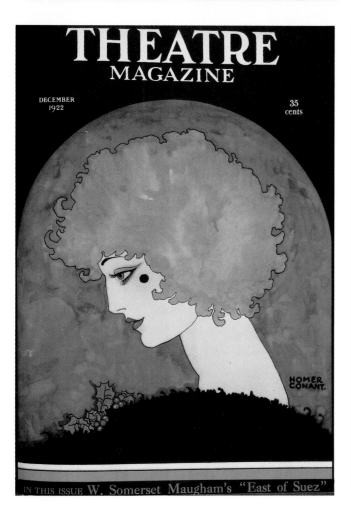

Theatre Magazine

MAY, 1922

TITLE REG. U.S. PAT. OFF.

35 cents

The early covers of *Theatre* (which added *Magazine* to its name in 1917) were chromolithographs based on photographs by Napoleon Sarony and others. They usually featured an actor or actress from a current Broadway success. Later covers displayed fanciful, nonspecific designs reflecting the editors' decision to include between the covers movies and other popular entertainment. In January 1926, Katharine Cornell landed on *Theatre Magazine*'s cover, having achieved notoriety in *The Green Hat,* a play of tainted love among the English upper classes. Her green hat became the fashion rage of that year. Opposite: covers of *Theatre Magazine* for January, March, and December 1922 and for January 1926. Left: May 1922

For five cents, one could buy *The Cast,* a turn-of-the-century weekly that included everything under the sun about the amusements in New York. Not only did it list the casts of every show in town but there were also short articles about happenings and notable personalities. Shown here is the cover of the issue dated August 11, 1902, which features vaudevillian Valerie Bergere

Journal des sçavans (1665–1792) for getting the idea rolling. From 1704 to 1713, Defoe was the publisher and editor of the *Review,* as well as its sole contributor. His success spurred many others to give vent to their political and intellectual itches in printed form.

The term *magazine* entered our vocabulary via Edward Cave's *Gentleman's Magazine.* In 1731 Cave, a London printer and bookseller, gathered the best of what was then appearing in a plethora of publications into a kind of high-class eighteenth-century *Reader's Digest.* By so doing, he hoped to preserve them permanently in his literary storehouse, or magazine. The concept jumped the ocean rather quickly. In 1741 Benjamin Franklin, the original compleat American, brought out not quite the first magazine in the colonial boondocks (he was scooped by Andrew Bradford's short-lived *American Magazine*). But Franklin had the satisfaction of seeing his weekly *General Magazine* endure throughout the momentous decades of the century. Like Defoe's *Review*, Franklin's magazine stimulated a host of imitations—nearly a hundred—which George Washington described as "easy vehicles of knowledge."

In 1798 the first magazine devoted to the theater made its appearance in the new nation. The *Thespian Oracle; or, Monthly Mirror, Consisting of Original Pieces and Selections from Performances of Merit, Relating Chiefly to the Most Admired Dramatic Compositions and Interspersed with Theatrical Anecdotes,* its title apparently doubling as table of contents, came out not in New York but in Philadelphia, the center of important theatrical events during most of the eighteenth century. Unhappily, it did not survive the first issue.

It is almost possible to read the history of the American theater in the history of the American theatrical magazine. The emergence of New York as the theatrical capital of the land very nearly coincided with the founding in the Empire City in 1831 of a publication, part newspaper and part magazine, that combined theatrical and sporting pages in a strange but apparently durable symbiosis. The *Spirit of the Times: A Chronicle of the Turf, Agriculture, Field Sports, Literature and the Stage* appeared to be exactly right for its age. Under a succession of publishers and editors, beginning with William Porter and James Howe, the *Spirit of the Times* endured throughout the century, ending its publication in 1902.

In 1853 another weekly, the *New York Clipper,* arrived on the scene to become the *Spirit*'s principal rival. But in addition to its weekly numbers, the *Clipper* published a sporting and theatrical annual. Descriptions of Charlotte Cushman's dramatic triumphs were followed by records of aquatic, track and field, and horse-racing feats. During the late 1860s, the *Clipper* acquired its most famous editor, Colonel T. Allston Brown, who chronicled the New York stage in several volumes, presumably in his spare time. One of the last historical links with the *Clipper* was severed upon the death of the Broadway producer Herman Shumlin, an old *Clipper* reporter, in 1979. In 1924, *Variety* absorbed the magazine sans its sports pages.

The last of the great American nineteenth-century theatrical weeklies was the *New York Dramatic Mirror,* which began publication in 1879 and managed to survive until 1922 without the customary sports coverage. In 1881 the *Dramatic Mirror* was acquired by the twenty-year-old theater-fixated Harrison Grey Fiske. Under his aegis the magazine found a *cause célèbre* in the monopoly known as the Theatrical Syndicate, presided over by Abraham Lincoln Erlanger

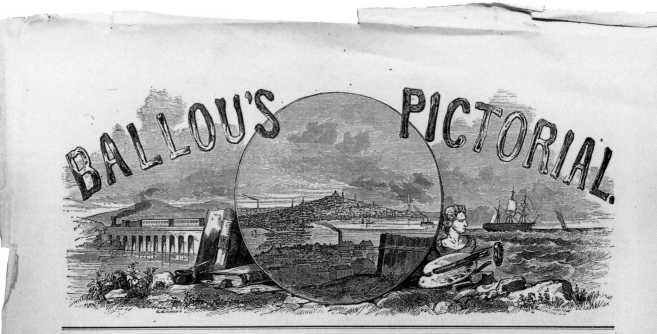

BALLOU'S PICTORIAL.

M. M. BALLOU, { CORNER OF TREMONT AND BROMFIELD STS. BOSTON, SATURDAY, FEBRUARY 24, 1855. $3,00 PER ANNUM. 6 CENTS SINGLE. { VOL. VIII., No. 8.—WHOLE No. 190.

NIBLO'S THEATRE, NEW YORK.

The accompanying engraving is an accurate representation of the interior of Niblo's well-known theatre, sketched on a recent opera night, showing the house crowded with spectators, and the stage set for a scene of Masaniello, with the fisherman and Fenella on the stage. Mr. Niblo has been identified with the amusements of New York for many years, and not to know Niblo's Garden is to be ignorant of one of the most popular places in the imperial city. The interior is very brilliantly decorated. The ceiling is in the form of a dome, painted in fresco, with gilded mouldings and carved trusses, the decorations consisting of alternate panel work and medallions. The front of the dress circle of boxes is ornamented with panels, the moulded edges of which are richly gilt. The front of the second tier of boxes is ornamented with highly finished medallions and figures in bas relief, and to this row twenty five chandeliers are attached by gilded branches. The upper row of boxes is also richly ornamented with wreaths of flowers in alto relief, carved busts, etc. The gold of the ornamentation is relieved by a groundwork of delicate rose color. The columns which support the upper row of boxes have gilded capitals and bases. The proscenium, an important feature in a theatre,—one side of which is shown in our engraving,—is very graceful in its design and finish. On either side a light and lofty arch springs from a solid base enclosing a private box. A caryatid of life size, on each side of this box supports a handsome pediment, on which rest two cupids in high relief. Above each pediment is another private box, decorated in the same style, and terminated in a richly moulded and heavily gilt cornice, from which springs the arch of the proscenium, having a span of fifty-four feet at its base. The decorations of the arch are in strict harmony with those of the ceiling. A medallion in high relief forms the centrepiece, and the oblong panels on either side are painted in fresco, with crimson borders, and rich ornaments, dead gilt. There are a number of private boxes draped with lace curtains. The seats throughout the house are furnished with hair stuffed spring cushions and backs, covered with maroon-colored velvet plush. In a word, no expense has been spared, to render this establishment elegant and attractive. Like all Mr. Niblo's undertakings, this new and gorgeous theatre has been eminently successful.

INTERIOR VIEW OF NIBLO'S THEATRE, NEW YORK.

THE BROOKLYN ACADEMY OF MUSIC.—EXTERIOR.—[SEE PAGE 78.]

ten me, Jeanie?"—really a very absurd question, and quite malapropos.

"No, indeed!"

"I thought you would"—really a very untrue statement.

"Did you? Oh, Fay!"

"I thought you wished to."

"And you hated me?"

"No, Jeanie, just the opposite—always!"

"And you could forgive me?"

"I hardly know which should forgive the other, Jeanie; but here, in this place, where we have so often listened together to the words of peace, is it not well for us to make our peace?"

She gave him her hand, quickly and silently, as

they bent over their evergreens, and the spirit of the olden time came back to them, hallowed, chastened, and made earnest by the grief through which they had passed.

On Christmas morning all the good people of

THE BROOKLYN ACADEMY OF MUSIC.—INTERIOR.　OPENING CONCERT ON TUESDAY, JANUARY 15, 1861.—[SEE PAGE 78.]

Opposite:

Ballou's Pictorial, emanating from Boston during the mid-nineteenth century, did not fail to cover the theatrical scene. To such illustrated magazines of the day we are indebted for pictures of the interiors of theaters not hitherto captured by the camera. The text accompanying this engraving observes of New York's landmark theater "not to know Niblo's Garden is to be ignorant of one of the most popular places in the imperial city"

Harper's Weekly marked the occasion of the opening of the Brooklyn Academy of Music by including engravings of both the exterior and the interior, thus providing theatrical and architectural historians with documentation concerning this still-standing hall, built in 1861 during an explosion in theater building in America

NEW YORK CLIPPER
THE OLDEST
AMERICAN SPORTING AND THEATRICAL JOURNAL.
NEW YORK, SATURDAY, JUNE 30, 1866.

NEW YORK CLIPPER
THE OLDEST AMERICAN SPORTING AND THEATRICAL JOURNAL.
NEW YORK, SATURDAY, FEBRUARY 8, 1890.

The journalistic banner most familiar to theatrical professionals during the second half of the nineteenth century was the *New York Clipper*. On the front page of an 1866 edition of the *Clipper* (left) was an engraving of a familiar face, the actor-manager John Brougham, who delighted several generations of New York theatergoers. The *Clipper*'s banner in 1890 (right) reflects a typographical change and suggests the presence of competition in its more prominently featured subtitle: *The Oldest American Sporting and Theatrical Journal*

and Marc Klaw, the evil geniuses of the scheme. From 1896 until 1911, when Fiske left the paper, he crucified the Syndicate in every issue. For many years, Fiske's offices were next door to the Empire Theatre, headquarters of the production offices of the Syndicate under Charles Frohman. Once when, inevitably, Fiske encountered Abe Erlanger on the sidewalk they shared, harsh words were exchanged and fists began to fly. Yet, despite the acrimony and the libel suits, when Fiske went broke years later it was the firm of Klaw and Erlanger that offered to tide him over.

The *Spirit,* the *Clipper,* and the *Dramatic Mirror* carried play reviews, commentaries, biographies, personal notices, obituaries, advertisements, feature articles on a full range of theatrical subjects, and editorials. Frequently they included illustrations, mainly drawings of performers or buildings, and occasionally cartoons. Although quartered in New York, they were national publications, and that was reflected in their coverage of events from coast to coast.

The phenomenon of theatrical publishing was and continues to be *Variety,* which owes its longevity to the ability of its various publishers to gauge and focus quickly on the dominant entertainment medium at any given moment. Founded in 1905 by Sime Silverman as a five-cent weekly, *Variety* began by reporting news and reviews of vaudeville, Sime's and apparently everyone else's favorite form of theater at the time. An untutored writer, Silverman was not only its publisher but also its editor, principal critic, and chief contributor rolled up in one. For twenty-four years *Variety* barely remained afloat, but Silverman's tenacity began to pay dividends in advertising pages and the gradual, if sometimes grudging, support of the industry.

Sime's "plain English" of the early years was slowly and deliberately replaced by a jargon full of ellipses (*H'wood*), abbreviations (*biz*), and Broadway colloquialisms. Some of *Variety*'s headlines have passed into American social history: "Wall Street Lays an Egg" (after the 1929 stock-market crash) and "Sticks Nix Hick Pix" (above a report on the unexpected popularity of sophisticated film fare in the midwestern boondocks). From the 1920s to 1987, *Variety* was quartered in the heart of the theater district in New York, on West Forty-sixth Street, with offices in Hollywood, Toronto, and Paris—a Silverman always at its head. But things, alas, have

The Theatre: A Record of the Stage made its debut on March 20, 1886, as a weekly, endeavoring "to provide the public with a bright and interesting paper containing certain features, which will...make it a useful and welcome visitor." From its birth to its expiration (in 1893), the editor was Deshler Welch. The magazine's topicality is reflected in this page from the November 22, 1886, issue celebrating the Statue of Liberty, notice of which had obviously been taken in contemporary minstrel acts changed. Both its weekly New York and daily West Coast editions were sold to the Cahners Publishing Company, and the New York office was moved to Park Avenue South, a spiritual continent away from the theater district. Syd Silverman, Sime's grandson, remains as of now as executive editor and publisher of the *Weekly Variety* and president of *Daily Variety*, but he presides over an entirely different theatrical newspaper. Today, *Variety*'s pages are filled with stories about television, films, cable, radio, and the recording industry, with a scant few pages devoted to news of the legitimate stage. Given its savvy responsiveness to the winds of change, *Variety* should go on forever, with or without the Silvermans.

At mid-nineteenth century, the cheap, heavily illustrated general interest counterpart of the *Illustrated London News* reached America with *Gleason's Pictorial and Drawing Room Companion, Frank Leslie's Illustrated Weekly,* and all of Leslie's later brainchildren. Later in the century, this type of publication found its paradigm in *Harper's Weekly,* which published wonderful engravings from drawings by the likes of Winslow Homer and included theatrical iconography along with theatrical news from home and abroad. The illustrations were all line engravings, which depended heavily on the skill of engravers for verisimilitude and were usually of very high quality. The time was quickly approaching, however, when photographic images could be transferred effectively to the printing plate. With the perfection of the halftone process about the turn of the century, the era of the specialty illustrated magazine was launched.

The single most important and influential theatrical magazine of its time, and the closest thing to a magazine of record for an entire era, is *Theatre,* which grew out of a picture book, *Our Players' Gallery,* in 1900. It was published by the brothers Meyer—Louis and Paul—and was edited for twenty-six years by Arthur Hornblow, Sr. It had only two other editors before it ceased publication (a victim of the Depression) in 1931: Perriton Maxwell, who had begun writing for the magazine in 1916 before becoming its editor in 1929, and Stewart Beach, the editor at its demise. Ada Patterson, the chief feature writer, began her career with the magazine in 1903 and was still on the staff at the end.

In the late nineteenth century, the *New York Clipper*'s chief competition came from the *New York Dramatic Mirror,* which was devoted exclusively to news of the theatrical rialto from coast to coast. During the editorial tenure of Harrison Grey Fiske, bitter enemy of the Theatrical Syndicate, it was once banned from all theaters controlled by producers Marc Klaw and Abraham Erlanger, Syndicate masterminds

---

THE NEW YORK DRAMATIC MIRROR.

VOL. XXIII., No. 579.   NEW YORK: SATURDAY, FEBRUARY 1, 1890.   PRICE TEN CENTS.

THE DRAMATIC MILLENNIUM

BY HENRY GUY CARLETON

After reading with conscientious industry

This may explain why Ibsen—but that is irrelevant.

A play is not a conversation, nor a beer-garden, nor a Sunday-school lecture, nor an object lesson in didactics; but a verisimilitude of human life, with diverse human interests and human emotions tangled in one

his grapes shall be crushed, but that the preciousness thereof may be divided from the pulp, and gladden the sons of men.

The young critic of the millennium will caution the hen that cackles in his garden that before accepting a chair of theology she should at least learn the right way and the

A ROMANCE OF THE STAGE.

It is a story, strange but true, of young love at first sight; the ages added of the two, make sixteen—if we're right. Actors juvenile they are, of fame and beauty rare; he owns a mass of flaxen locks, and she has raven hair.

THEATRE MAGAZINE

Vol. XXXV No. 252   MARCH, 1922

Photo Abbe

Richard Bennett As the Clown In Andreyev's Drama
"He Who Gets Slapped"

[141]

Theatre (which changed its name to *Theatre Magazine* with the August 1917 issue) had modest aims. Editor Hornblow stated them in the first issue: "to put before the public in an attractive form all that is going on in the sister worlds of Drama and Music, the text being profusely illustrated with fine reproductions of photographs of scenes from plays and operas, and of artistes." The policy of the magazine, couched in wonderful and self-righteous Victorian prose, was to "approve and encourage everything that tends to elevate the tone of the stage and add to the dignity of the profession of the artistes." Further, it intended to praise good work and "censure fearlessly where Art has been trampled and debased." And throughout its history, the magazine lived up to its promises. It *was* profusely illustrated, keeping busy, each in its time, the leading theatrical photo studios of Byron, White, and Vandamm and featuring scenes from plays and operas and portraits of "artistes." It was printed on slick, coated stock in a large-page format with full-color chromolithographic covers, usually featuring, in photographs or

James Abbe (1883–1973) was one of many photographers whose work was regularly published in *Theatre Magazine* during the 1920s. Abbe took photo portraits of hundreds of theater and film stars. The magazine made his shot of Richard Bennett an elaborate presentation in their March 1922 issue

In addition to informative articles about the stage, *Theatre* also included cartoons, poetry, and fanciful little pieces like this one by a Broadway costume designer in the May 1922 issue. Although the Roaring Twenties were barely launched, Charles Le Maire's figures mirror the quintessential look of the decade

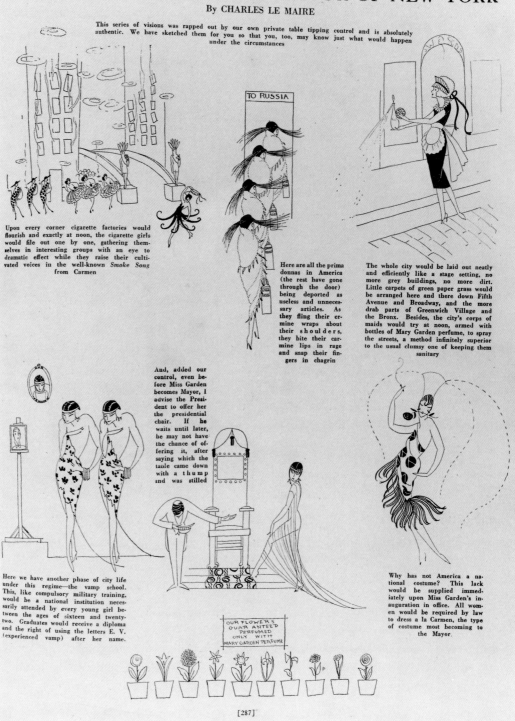

Theatre Magazine, May, 1922

IF MARY GARDEN WERE MAYOR OF NEW YORK
By CHARLES LE MAIRE

This series of visions was rapped out by our own private table tipping control and is absolutely authentic. We have sketched them for you so that you, too, may know just what would happen under the circumstances

Upon every corner cigarette factories would flourish and exactly at noon, the cigarette girls would file out one by one, gathering themselves in interesting groups with an eye to dramatic effect while they raise their cultivated voices in the well-known *Smoke Song* from Carmen

TO RUSSIA

Here are all the prima donnas in America (the rest have gone through the door) being deported as useless and unnecessary articles. As they fling their ermine wraps about their s h o u l d e r s, they bite their carmine lips in rage and snap their fingers in chagrin

The whole city would be laid out neatly and efficiently like a stage setting, no more grey buildings, no more dirt. Little carpets of green paper grass would be arranged here and there down Fifth Avenue and Broadway, and the more drab parts of Greenwich Village and the Bronx. Besides, the city's corps of maids would try at noon, armed with bottles of Mary Garden perfume, to spray the streets, a method infinitely superior to the usual clumsy one of keeping them sanitary

And, added our control, even before Miss Garden becomes Mayor, I advise the President to offer her the presidential chair. If he waits until later, he may not have the chance of offering it, after saying which the table came down with a t h u m p and was stilled

Here we have another phase of city life under this regime—the vamp school. This, like compulsory military training, would be a national institution necessarily attended by every young girl between the ages of sixteen and twenty-two. Graduates would receive a diploma and the right of using the letters E. V. (experienced vamp) after her name.

OUR FLOWERS GUAR ANTEED PERFUMED ONLY WITH MARY GARDEN PERFUME

Why has not America a national costume? This lack would be supplied immediately upon Miss Garden's inauguration in office. All women would be required by law to dress a la Carmen, the type of costume most becoming to the Mayor.

[287]

original artwork, a star of the season in a current role. The thin early issues, sold at twenty-five cents per copy, grew thicker as the magazine established itself and attracted more and more advertising. When it finally settled into an acceptable format, it included such regular departments as editorials, book reviews, play reviews ("Mr. Hornblow Goes to the Play"), letters to the editor, notes on fashions, historical and nostalgic articles, reports on what was going on abroad, puff pieces on stage stars and personalities, and even a dash of poetry now and then. There were some arty pictures by its contributing photographers, among whom were Francis

Bruguière, James Pondelicek, and Maurice Goldberg. Line drawings, caricatures (early Al Hirschfelds, among others), and silhouettes were also included from time to time.

Hornblow and his successors took their mission seriously and swept as much as they could between the covers of the magazine. *Theatre* was never meant to be controversial, although Hornblow took up cudgels in the service of a few causes. One of them was censorship. While he came out swinging against official censorship, threatened from time to time, he pleaded with producers to police their own naughty productions to avoid government intervention. When something on stage offended him, he used the magazine as the forum for his disgust. In 1907 he trounced a production of Richard Strauss's *Salome* at the Metropolitan so mercilessly that the opera was pulled from the repertory. He printed articles by producers who decried the current preoccupation of playwrights with subjects of the gutter and urged Actors' Equity Association to discountenance performances in which its members were asked to remove their clothes onstage. (This was in the roaring, amoral 1920s!) When the motion-picture industry set up its own censorship committee, he strongly suggested that stage producers follow suit. For Hornblow, elevating the tone of the American theater meant cleaning it up, but it also represented a return to the classics and serious drama. If he ever felt he was waging a losing battle, the stream of articles from his pen belied it.

Hornblow wanted to see an endowed national theater established and tried to enlist the support of important theatrical figures—to no avail. Taking a strange model, he praised Mussolini for making Luigi Pirandello the head of Italian theater! With unflagging zeal, he attacked ticket speculators; he urged theater owners to make their playhouses safer; he criticized critics; he pleaded for better diction from actors; he railed against the bad manners of audiences; and he advanced what must be the prototype of the current Broadway Mall concept, the closing of the Great White Way to all but streetcars at show time.

To keep abreast of the times, a department devoted entirely to motion pictures was added in 1917. The magazine also included news of high-school, college, community, and "art" theaters, first referred to as "amateur," later as "tributary" theater. *Theatre Magazine* never sank to a gossip column, but an occasional "personal item" was slipped into an editorial or feature article.

The magazine died a victim of the times and a change in theatrical taste. Its conservatism, its lack of enthusiasm for the new dramaturgy (propounded by Eugene O'Neill), and the new trends in stagecraft, along with the rise of *Theatre Arts* magazine, all contributed to its sad demise. As a chronicle of the theater of its day, with allowances made for its prejudices, *Theatre/Theatre Magazine* provides significant insights into the American stage as it came of age.

Theatre was the unapologetic reflection of establishment theater of its day, but the little magazine that was launched in 1916 in Detroit with the sponsorship of the Detroit Society of Arts and Crafts was dedicated from the start to a loftier mission than the entertainment of its readers and coverage of Broadway. Sheldon Cheney, founder and first editor of *Theatre Arts*, designed the publication "for the artist who approaches the theater in the spirit of the arts and crafts movement and for the theatregoer who is awake artistically and intellectually." To them, he offered it as a "forum for the expression of original ideas." Cheney disdained commercial

A perennial feature of *Theatre* was "Mr. Hornblow Goes to the Play," in which the longtime editor Arthur Hornblow, Sr. aired his views on the current offerings. Readers were meant to pay attention to the expression on the face of the little top-hatted figure as a clue to his assessment. He is all smiles on this page from the July 1926 issue

---

Mr. Hornblow Goes to the Play

Watch the Expression on His Face

THE play advertised as *The Importance of Being Earnest* should have read *Ernest*, for that is how Oscar Wilde wrote it, intending to convey that this particular Christian name had an important bearing on his plot; two of his characters, John and Algernon, having masqueraded under this name to win their respective sweethearts. Revived at the Comedy by the Actors' Theatre, it revealed once more its brittle and unsubstantial, yet often corruscating qualities. The play is partly comedy and partly farce. It would not be fair to say it creaks with age. It has as much value to-day as it had years ago, but it is that value itself which is debatable. It is just an artificial trifle. The characters indulge in verbal fireworks and constantly echo the author's own quizzical vagaries and never their own personalities. It is so flimsy in story that it can hardly be called a play at all. But it amuses those who can find enjoyment in purely literary pyrotechnics.

The performance on the whole was excellent. With the exception of Dudley Digges, who as the parson either neglected or misunderstood his part in performing his well-executed duties as stage director, and Lucile Watson, who, though a facile performer, entirely failed to portray the dignity of Lady Bracknell, the cast revealed much dexterity. Reginald Owen fairly shone as Algernon. He gave a type of the insipid, though sapient Britisher, which was delightful, and Haroldine Humphreys as Gwendolen contributed a charm of bearing and a clearness of utterance that gave added value to the play. Patricia Collinge as Cicely showed her usual technical skill, but she lacked Miss Humphrey's illuminating diction. Catherine Proctor played the governess with complete understanding. To Vernon Steele was assigned what might be called the hero of the story, if we grant that a story so slight can have a hero. As John Worthing he showed all the intelligence necessary, though he lacked in buoyancy. Without this latter quality, Wilde becomes rather a bore.

THE Neighborhood Players presented May 4 a delightful little comedy, translated from the Spanish of G. Martinez Sierra by Helen and H. Granville Barker, called *The Romantic Young Lady*. The title did not seem quite so apposite as the original *Sueña de una noche de Agosta*, for it is during a night in August that the half-droll, half-sentimental incidents of the little play occur.

The real value of this unpretentious comedy was ably set forth by Mr. Barker in a little essay printed in the program. Señor Sierra is

a dramatist who does not consider himself superior to the recognized canons of play-writing. He contrives, with ample knowledge of the theatre, scenes that have inherent dramatic interest, and he clothes them in appropriate dialogue. The latter is always natural, and the humor flows spontaneously and is never of that artificial quality that obtains in the Oscar Wilde output. The story may be slight, but it is always entertaining, and the response from the audience clearly indicated that the choice of this play for the talents of the Neighborhood company was a wise one.

Plays You Ought to See

BRIDE OF THE LAMB—An exceptionally interesting and forceful play of religious fanaticism and suppressed desire. Well acted by Alice Brady, Wilbur Crane and competent cast.

CRAIG'S WIFE—Comedy of a domestic tyrant. Only fair to middling as a play, but carried to success by splendid performance of Chrystal Herne as the shrewish wife. Won Pulitzer Prize for 1925.

H. M. S. PINAFORE—Brilliant revival of the famous Gilbert and Sullivan operetta with Fay Templeton, Marguerite Namara, John E. Hazzard, Charles Galagher and other favorites in the principal rôles.

IOLANTHE—Another delightful Gilbert and Sullivan revival. Amusing, charming and tuneful, with Ernest Lawford, John Barclay, Vera Ross and Lois Bennett.

JUNO AND THE PAYCOCK—Remarkable study of Irish life by Sean O'Casey. Produced in America for the first time. Pathos and humor combine to make a fine play.

THE LAST OF MRS. CHEYNEY—Smart and entertaining crook play, with Ina Claire as a girl thief who wins her way in society.

YOUNG WOODLEY—Charming comedy of English school life, with Glenn Hunter as a dreaming schoolboy, and a wonderful performance by Helen Gahagan as the master's wife.

It afforded especially fine opportunities for Ian MacLaren as a romantic intruder in the household of the fair Rosario on an August night, and gave Mary Ellis as Rosario ample scope for a charming, persuasive and highly intelligent performance of a Spanish maiden enmeshed in the baffling impulses of a first love. Mr. MacLaren, seeking shelter from a storm, climbs through an open window at midnight and finds Rosario reading a novel. In the ensuing panic the maiden's tresses become ensnared in the intruder's sleeve-links, and a very deft scene of comedy results from the attempts of both to become disentangled.

A certain intimacy is, of course, immediately engendered from this brief but enforced proximity, and in this intimacy the intruder learns that Rosario is very much enamored of the author of the book she has been reading and thankfully accepts the intruder's offer of a personal letter of introduction to him. Naturally the novelist and the intruder prove to be one and the same.

There is little attempt made to mystify the audience. This is no cheap mystery play. But the outcome of the love affair thus projected is

followed by the audience with much interest and delight, and the final proposal of marriage is handled with great cleverness and originality.

Assisting in these diverting proceedings is Rosario's grandmother (charmingly played by Dorothy Sands), who having married and buried three husbands, may be fairly called an expert in the art of love. Another fine performance is given by Paula Truesman as the author's private secretary.

A MEATY British comedy, seen at the Lyceum, is *The Sport of Kings*, by Major Ian Hay Beith, immortally noted for his humorous masterpiece, "The First Hundred Thousand." I am told that Major Beith's latest offering to public laughter has had a substantial success in England. There is no reason why that success might not have been duplicated here, had the piece been produced with professional competence. Amateur buffooning did massacre to a comedy fragile in its story and delicate in its dialogue for all the broad and frequently burlesque farce that composed it.

The story is suggestive of Pinero's *The Magistrate*. It finds the home of Amos Purdie, J. P., invaded by two young race-track followers, who seek a residence near the course. Mr. Purdie is the essence of Puritanism, decrying racing and its allied vices. He rides his unfortunate wife and his two children with a rule of righteousness. Major Beith's play concerns itself with the efforts of our two young men in converting the revered J. P. to a new faith in humanity in general and horse-racing in particular. They succeed so well that before the final curtain is down Mr. Purdie has turned bookie.

Here certainly is no great or novel entertainment. But the Beith wit rode lightly over the old plot and there was fun aplenty. Not enough, however, to raise it from the doldrums of bad casting and the worst direction a play has had this season. The veteran O. P. Heggie, so good in that other Beith comedy, *Happy Go Lucky* (*née Tillie of Bloomsbury*), was mildly amusing as the sanctimonious Purdie, but his performance savored more of burlesque than a legitimate characterization. Alan Mowbray, an English actor, did well as Sprigge, one of the racing men who invade the J. P.'s home, and Betty Lilley and Alison Bradshaw invested with beauty and charm their respective rôles of Dulcie and Katie.

A PLEASANT little play, entitled *Friend Indeed* and accredited to Clayton Hamilton and Bernhard Voigt, was tentatively exhibited at the Central Park Theatre, which is the rather ornate title of a little lecture-room on West

15

---

theater, particularly the sentimental realistic plays purveyed by playwright-producer David Belasco, and promised that the magazine would not be "swallowed by the movies." By the time *Theatre Arts* reached its peak, Cheney and his successors were forced to swallow many of their words.

Theatre Arts at once became the voice of experimental theater throughout the country, a fortuitous circumstance for the little art theaters springing up everywhere, because the magazine gave them a dignity and importance that they would not have had otherwise. Cheney gave them, their producers, their founders, their playwrights, their designers, and their innovators a forum for their ideas. A fine writer himself, he published perceptive and often brilliant articles written by O'Neill, Robert Edmond Jones, Sam Hume, Kenneth Macgowan, Percy MacKaye, Thomas Wood Stevens, Ruth St. Denis, Maurice Browne, all of whom were involved in the little theater movement, and by budding critics Walter Prichard Eaton, John Mason Brown, and Ashley Dukes, and a host of others. When Edith Isaacs became editor in

1922, she paid homage to Cheney's pioneering spirit, noting that he had started the magazine when "there were not a half a dozen men in America writing intelligently about the theater; there were not half a dozen designers whose work was worth note; not half a dozen adventurous producers to start on their way the playwrights that now double their number each year to make one large creative group." By putting them and their ideas into print, Cheney provided a telling assist to the maturing of American theater.

Theatre Arts began as an illustrated quarterly, but the pictures were not the usual stuff of fan magazines. Scene designs and costume sketches, moody photographs of experimental productions, and an occasional caricature (even if not published with the best reproduction) form an excellent visual record of many early productions for which many of the original graphics have not survived. Although the illustrations appeared in black-and-white, written descriptions many times indicate the colors that were used for sets and costumes.

From time to time, a short play or an excerpt from a longer play was included in the magazine's pages, along with poetry; reviews of plays and books; articles on ballet, children's theater, the circus, theatrical history, audiences, puppet theater, opera, and radio; and always reports on theater throughout the world. A year after its establishment, Cheney moved from Detroit to New York. He had recently published an article praising German experimental theater and, America having just thrown in her lot with the Allies, the Detroit Society of Arts and Crafts was not pleased. Dependent for survival on subscribers and a limited number of institutional and professional advertisers, the magazine skated on very thin ice during its first decade.

In its pages, month after month, *Theatre Magazine* included light and airy articles about doings on Broadway, frequently accompanied by photographs or drawings. This page from the May 1922 issue, featuring "The Promenades of Angelina" and drawings by Artel, describes the rehearsal of a play starring Marjorie Rambeau

THEATRE ARTS

April 1957

Fifty Cents

José Quintero — director of hit productions of two plays by Eugene O'Neill.

The simple wrappers of the original *Theatre Arts,* the voice of the experimental theater, slowly gave way to colorful and individualized covers more reflective of establishment theater, which it eventually came to represent. Caricaturist Al Hirschfeld's drawing on the April 1957 cover shows Eugene O'Neill pulling strings from aloft to manipulate José Quintero, the director of two of the late dramatist's plays

©Al Hirschfeld. Drawing reproduced by special arrangement with Hirschfeld's exclusive representative, The Margo Feiden Galleries, New York

Opposite:

The covers for *Show* were invariably distinctive. The January 1963 issue featured the boys from the hit musical *Oliver!* in a photograph taken by Frances McLaughlin-Gill

In 1923 *Theatre Arts* went monthly, under Edith Isaacs. She also made an attempt to include a full-length play in each issue. Under her aegis, as it matured, *Theatre Arts* moved ever closer to the mainstream. Attacks on commercial theater became muted, and in 1931 the magazine did a complete turnabout. Once the butt of its editorial scorn, Belasco, recently deceased, was held up as a shining example of theatrical professionalism: "It would be well for every young worker in the theatre to study the fifty years of Belasco's active experience, to get the background of this craft." Movies began to receive attention and ultimately gained their own department, while the amateur and little theaters were relegated to a monthly column called "Tributary Theatre," a term unconsciously borrowed from *Theatre Magazine*. The illustrations, still heavily focused on costume and scene designs, began to include more and more pictures of stars and scenes from plays and movies. Color was added, and advertisements for cosmetics, cars, hotels, and Broadway shows reflected the influence of New York. The simple, understated covers of the early years became colorful and by the mid-1940s featured a Broadway star or a scene from a show.

Isaacs remained editor until 1945, when Rosamond Gilder, one of the associate editors, assumed the post. In 1948 Alexander Sandor Ince merged *Theatre Arts* with *Stage,* a one-time rival publication that had ended its run in 1939, and made the Broadway playwright Charles MacArthur the editor of the combined *Theatre Arts Magazine*. During the merger, there were skipped issues, which bespoke internal adjustments. Then, in January 1949, John MacArthur, business tycoon and older brother of Charles, was listed as publisher. From this point on, there was no ambiguity in the policy of the magazine: it would be devoted to the

SHOW

Incorporating USA*1

THE
MAGAZINE
OF
THE ARTS

75 CENTS
JANUARY 1963

THE KIDS FROM
"OLIVER!"
BRITAIN LOOKS IN
ON BROADWAY

"THE TIN DRUM"
GERMANY'S
SENSATIONAL
NEW NOVEL

WESTBROOK PEGLER
ON BOXING'S
GREAT SHOWMEN

Above:

Because its principal audience is "professionals in theatre, film, video, and the performing arts" and because it seeks a national base, *Theatre Crafts* chooses not to be parochial, extending its coverage to regional and university theater and kindred arts. It cannot, however, afford to neglect Broadway, America's theatrical matrix. Pictured on the cover in August–September 1984 was leading actor Mandy Patinkin against the set of *Sunday in the Park with George.* That issue highlights the scenery and lighting of the award-winning Broadway production

Above right:

In November 1987, *American Theatre,* a recent entry into competition for the attention of theater buffs, carried a price of $3.50 and a UPC symbol—both signs of the times. National in its scope, it frequently features on its covers performers from re-gional theater. Here shown are Daniel Davis and Caroline Lagerfelt in a production of Molière's *The Misanthrope* at the Guthrie Theatre in Minneapolis

Right:

One can only admire the courage of the publishers of the infant *Theater Week* for launching another magazine for and about the American theater when so many others have failed. Still feeling their way in the field, the editors cover both Broadway and Off Broadway in their pages and have cut the format from tabloid to magazine. Because it is a weekly, the publication can zoom in on the latest important happening. The October 23, 1988, issue featured the new A. R. Gurney, Jr. production, *The Cocktail Hour,* and its stars. Left to right: Bruce Davison, Nancy Marchand, Keene Curtis, Holland Taylor

commercial theater (on Broadway) and its betterment. Its new format, with slick paper stock and lots of color, more closely resembled the old *Stage* than the old *Theatre Arts*. The magazine made the publication of a full-length current play, a practice begun by *Stage*, part of its usual, not sometime, format and opened up its advertising space to all. Like *Theatre Magazine*, it attempted to include something for everyone, reporting on developments off Broadway and in the provinces. It strove mightily to be entertaining in a desperate attempt to keep in print.

When illness forced Charles MacArthur to retire from *Theatre Arts Magazine*, the editorship was assumed by Eileen Tighe, but by 1953 John MacArthur was entirely in charge, as both editor and publisher. In 1959 Peter J. Ryan was listed as publisher and Bruce Bohle as editor. The latter was shortly thereafter succeeded by Norman Zierold. In September 1962, Byron Bentley was the new editor and publisher and then, without much warning, *Theatre Arts Magazine* ceased publication with the January 1964 issue, nearly forty-eight years after it began life in Detroit, Michigan, as a herald of the insurgent theater.

There was much that was similar in the evolution of *Stage* and of *Theatre Arts*, suggesting that eventually the two might cross paths. The ancestor of *Stage* was also a little magazine, some twenty to thirty pages in length. It was brought out in November 1923 by an avant-garde group championed by Cheney, the newly founded Theatre Guild, one of whose directors, Lawrence Langner, launched its publication and served as its editor, promising that it would come out "occasionally." The occasional result was *Theatre Arts Bulletin*, which became a quarterly in 1925 and a monthly in 1928. Langner was succeeded by Hiram Moderwell (who later changed his name to Motherwell), and he attracted a host of contributors who looked very much like, and sometimes were the same as, the men and women who were writing for *Theatre Arts*. Although the magazine reflected the Theatre Guild's initial predilection for European drama and stagecraft, it gradually recognized the new energy in the emerging American theater in its pages.

In 1932 John Hanrahan of the *New Yorker* decided that *Theatre Arts Bulletin* could be more than a "house organ" of the Theatre Guild and had possibilities as a broad-interest theater magazine. Consequently, he took it over, changed its name to *Stage*, promising to add color and excitement to its pages. He also enlarged its scope to include the "cognate arts" of national and international motion pictures, music, radio, and dance. Hanrahan fulfilled all of his pledges— and then some. The magazine was printed on coated stock with full-color covers, lots of advertising, photographs, fashions, and a little gossip and incidental intelligence ("Claudette Colbert goes to Dorothy Gray Salon for facials when in New York"). Later a subtitle was added, *The Magazine of After Dark*, allowing the publisher to include nightclubs and just about anything left in the world of entertainment.

In 1939 the lingering effects of the Depression and a shrinking audience for live entertainment brought *Theatre Arts* and *Stage* to the brink of bankruptcy. Since they were covering much the same territory, survival went to the stronger of the two, and *Theatre Arts Magazine*, with the subsumed *Stage*, was able to hang on for the next twenty-five years.

Despite the downward course of live theater in the age of television and the dwindling subscriptions for theater magazines, millionaire Huntington Hartford decided in 1961 to launch a magazine, *Show*, which he hoped would "fill the void left by such as *Vanity Fair*" to become "an all embracing publication of culture and the arts, and particularly of the performing arts." It was big, elaborately produced, glitzy and gimmicky, and cost one dollar at the newsstands. It had Arthur Schlesinger, Jr. reviewing movies; Virgil Thomson reviewing music; and Jack Richardson reviewing theater. It roamed the world of letters to come up with such contributors as Max Lerner, Kenneth Tynan, Norman Podhoretz, and Al Capp. It had its pop side, with articles on Marilyn Monroe and Sophia Loren ("At Home with Sophia," by Carlo Ponti). There were lots of grainy photographs of performances in action and arty color work. In 1962, *Show* merged with Hugh Hefner's *Show Business Illustrated,* a similar, if not so glossily produced, magazine and took away its competition. In 1965 what was to be the "definitive" magazine of the performing arts cut its losses and quietly stopped the presses.

Perhaps a few more than seven hundred theatrical periodicals, in both magazine and newspaper formats, have come and gone in America since 1798, when the *Thespian Oracle* was born and died. Those that have survived have served very specialized audiences: actors and professionals; high-school and college drama departments; learned societies; avant-garde and little or provincial theaters; and scholars and critics of theatrical history. *Theatre Crafts,* founded in 1967 to cover technical aspects of university and professional theater, has achieved modest success with its limited focus. *American Theatre,* founded in 1984 as a "monthly forum for news, features and opinions," is a product of Theatre Communications Group, a broadly based service organization set up to assist regional theaters throughout the country. It tries to reflect the mission of its parent organization in reporting the news of its constituency. It has not neglected the general public in including articles of widespread interest, but it has yet to reach theatergoers and make itself felt in the world of professional theater. However, it is still too early to predict its future. It enjoys partial subsidy from its parent organization, a factor that may give it enough time to find its niche.

There have been and will continue to be attempts to revive the broad-based popular performing-arts magazine, but the sorry fact is that the audience is too small to offset the high costs of producing and distributing such a periodical. (Currently on the newsstands are *Playbill,* a monthly version of the Broadway theater program, which utilizes the format of its prototype minus the credits of the shows plus a different cover, and *Theater Week,* begun in 1987 as a newsy tabloid and aimed mainly at a New York audience.) The largest circulation in the history of serial publication has been achieved by the weekly *TV Guide,* a fact that speaks volumes about the state of entertainment today. In the absence of a theatrical magazine to serve what is left of the national theatergoing public, the slack has been taken up by the few remaining general-interest illustrated magazines and newspapers. They will probably continue to publish news of the rialto out of a sense of responsibility to history or their readers—or out of sentimentality for the fabulous invalid.

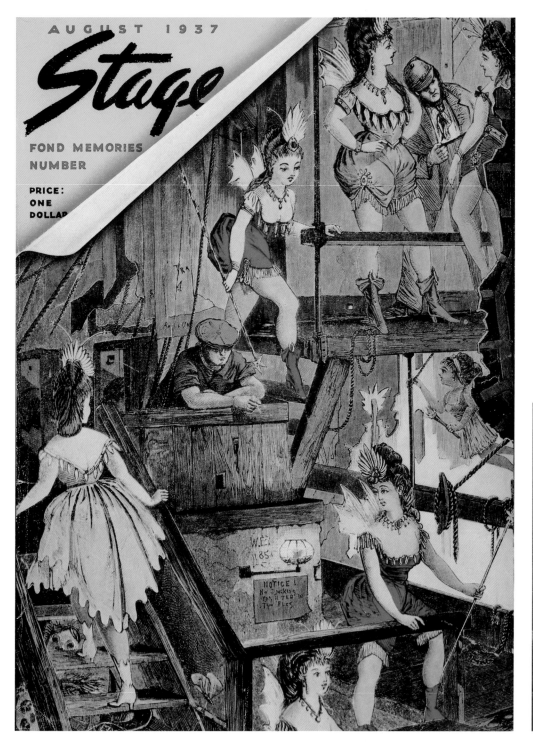

The August 1937 cover of *Stage* evoked the spirit of the nineteenth century with a reproduction of an engraving of activity behind the scenes at a performance of *The Black Crook*, a popular musical of 1866. Billed as the "Fond Memories Number," the issue was filled with nostalgic articles about the American theater of bygone eras

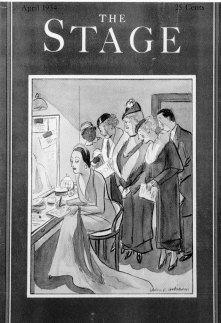

The short-lived *Stage* began as a general-interest theater magazine in 1932 and spent the next seven years in search of an audience. Its covers often featured drawings, such as this classic Helen Hokinson cartoon of matinee ladies (April 1934)

SEVENTY-FIVE CENTS   MAY 1962

THEATRE ARTS

THEATRE ARCHITECTURE

THE BRITISH SCENE

Complete Play: prior to Broadway

BILLY LIAR

ZERO MOSTEL

SHOW

THE
MAGAZINE
OF
THE
PERFORMING
ARTS

$1.00
NOVEMBER 1961

INSIDE: US
By S. J. Perelman

The editors of *Show* aimed to
please everyone by spreading the
subjects of their flashy covers
among the various visual and
performing arts. For the November
1961 issue, they chose that
icon of the Hollywood golden age
of movies Harpo Marx. The photograph
is from Dan Wynn

Opposite:

Zero Mostel's steady climb to
Broadway stardom was duly recognized
by *Theatre Arts* when
they featured the face of this
versatile performer on the May
1962 cover. Two years later, Mostel
was catapulted into superstardom
when he appeared as
Tevya in *Fiddler on the Roof*
(1964)

Caricatures

Theatrical photographers have given us, through the faithful eye of the camera, reflections of the American theater from the mid-nineteenth century onward. They recorded for posterity the faces of performers long gone and forgotten, and later they froze scenes from plays, capturing some qualities of the prevailing acting styles and conventions in scenery. Because photography continues to live on the brink of great expectations, it remains forever an exciting medium, in perfect harmony with the art of the theater. But there is another kind of chronicler of the theater, armed with pen and ink or pencil (and perhaps, a bit of acid), who provides us with a different kind of record: the caricaturist. His (or hers) is not a mirror image, not a calculated grab at reality, but a deliberately distorted vision of the pretensions of the theatrical world and its denizens. Theatrical caricature today is the almost exclusive province of Albert Hirschfeld. His work has had an incalculable impact on theatrical iconography and, it is probably safe to say, on the world of the theater itself. As anyone who has been his subject will attest, to be caricatured by Al Hirschfeld is the unrivaled mark of recognition. His worthy art has venerable roots in America and deserves a backward glance.

First a definition: *caricature* is derived from an Italian word for something that is overloaded or supercharged. William Auerbach-Levy, one of the towering figures of the genre, simply called it the art of exaggerated representation. As such, it is probably one of the oldest art forms in the world. When one of our early ancestors picked up a stick to draw in the dust a distorted picture of his enemy or an animal, he was creating the first caricature; when a schoolboy draws a nasty doodle of his teacher, he is carrying on the tradition. The gargoyle on the Gothic cathedral is a caricature expanded into three dimensions. From Leonardo to Picasso, the greatest artists have given vent to their anger or disgust or a desire to ridicule the human race through the caricature. Apparently, it is as natural an expression of Homo sapiens as the laugh, the tear, or the cheer. It is almost always deflating, which is why it works so well in the theatrical world, where massive egos are sometimes known to reside.

Ralph Barton (1891–1931) was practically reared in his mother's art studio in Kansas City. After some training at the Art Institute of Chicago, he went to work for the *Kansas City Star.* New York beckoned, and very quickly his caricatures were being published by *Puck, Life, Judge, Photoplay, Vanity Fair, Harper's Bazaar,* and, from 1925 to 1931, the *New Yorker.* A lifelong Francophile, Barton spent as much time in Paris as he did in New York. In addition to his caricatures, he painted the intermission drop curtain for Nikita Balieff's revue *Chauve-Souris* and did illustrations for Anita Loos's bestselling *Gentlemen Prefer Blondes* and *But Gentlemen Marry Brunettes.* After years of living the high life, he fell victim to melancholia and took his own life in 1931. His work was heavily influenced by the English caricaturists Max Beerbohm and Oliver Herford. Barton's odd assortment of characters in this undated drawing of yesteryear's "groupie," a sweet thing from Washington Square, set among George Bernard Shaw, Oscar Wilde, John Galsworthy, Anton Chekhov, Maurice Maeterlinck, James M. Barrie, David Belasco, Henrik Ibsen, Arthur Wing Pinero, and Eugène Brieux, covers the theatrical waterfront internationally

Left:

In her (unpublished) autobiography, Aline Fruhauf (1907–1978) told of her lifelong addiction, as she puts it, to "making faces" on any available surface. After study at Parsons School of Design and the Art Students League, she became a protégée of Ralph Barton, and with his assist her drawings began to appear in the *New York World* and popular magazines. After a few years of freelancing, she received commissions to produce drawings of fellow artists, fashion designers, musicians, authors, jurists, and politicians as well as theatrical personalities. She worked from life in pen and ink, dry brush, woodcut, lithography, watercolor, and every other medium that caught her fancy. In this watercolor, Fruhauf captures the fragility of Lillian Gish in her role in the 1930 Broadway production of Anton Chekhov's *Uncle Vanya* but, not forgetting the fundamental premise of her trade, she gives the actress an almost tipsy look

Above:

In 1921, Vincent Sardi, a former waiter at Rector's restaurant, the famous watering hole for a generation of stars and stargazers, set up his own spa with his wife on West Forty-fourth Street, in the heart of the theater district. Shortly after moving the restaurant to its present location in 1927, Sardi began posting Alex Gard caricatures on the wall, and the practice was carried on by his son and successor, Vincent Sardi, Jr. When Gard died in 1948, other caricaturists provided the service, notably John Mackey, Don Bevan, and Richard Baratz. Achieving immortality on a wall in Sardi's is an unspoken goal of many performers, producers, and prominent New Yorkers

The caricature got its greatest assist and widest dissemination through the printing press and its eventual offspring, the newspaper and the magazine. As a matter of fact, the word *caricature* first entered the language in a 1712 issue of the *Spectator*. During the eighteenth century, the new art form became a vehicle for political commentary both in England and in France. In England the names of William Hogarth and Isaac and George Cruikshank are eternally associated with it. In France in 1830 Charles Philipon used the fledgling medium of lithography to create the first illustrated comic newspaper, *Caricature*, for which he employed a string of artists, the greatest of whom was Honoré Daumier. When the paper was hounded out of circulation because of his ferocious political attacks on the government, Philipon responded by producing a successor, *Charivari*, whose name, derived from medieval Italian, denotes a street procession directed against an obnoxious neighbor, a kind of communal Bronx cheer. In 1842 *Charivari* was used as the subtitle for *Punch*, England's greatest comic illustrated magazine. *Punch: or, the London Charivari* did not confine itself to politics but made all of English society the butt of its swift and acerbic humor. The *Punch* caricature, far from offending, elevated its subject to the company of the immortals, as the hero of Mark Twain's "£1,000,000 Bank Note" observes.

> But mind, this was not fame, as yet I had achieved only notoriety; Then came the climaxing stroke—the accolade, so to speak—which in a single instant transmuted the perishable dross of notoriety into the enduring gold of fame: *Punch* caricatured me! Yes, I was a made man now; my place was established.

By the mid-nineteenth century, imitations of *Punch* flourished throughout Europe, but not until 1877 did the idea cross the Atlantic. It was introduced by an Austrian, Joseph Keppler, who arrived in America in 1868, planning to make his way in the theater. A notable lack of luck impelled him to revert to his original calling as an artist, for which he had trained at the Académie des Beaux-Arts in Vienna. He founded *Puck* and immediately hit pay dirt. In its peak years, Keppler hired a small army of illustrators for the magazine, some of whom went on to greater fame and fortune. Because of Keppler's interest in the theater, hardly an issue went by that did not include allusions to the stage and its folk: political figures, for example, were pictured as characters from Shakespeare or were shown ranting or posturing upon the boards. The success of *Puck* inspired imitations, and even the older, established magazines began to include cartoons and caricatures in their issues.

During the nineteenth century, actors, actresses, and other theatrical personalities were a constant source of material for caricaturists—for two reasons. First, they were (and continue to be) among the most public of public figures. The worshipful attention given to their most trivial acts, public or private, and their sometimes outrageous behavior both on and off the stage made them the true stuff of caricature. Second, officialdom and the clergy maintained a lingering hostility toward the theater. Suspicious of anything trivial or diverting or extravagant, the moralists, displaying the last vestiges of eighteenth-century American puritanism, had a field day in print with theater people. In *The Comic National History of the Human Race*, published in

1851, there is a portrait of America's first great star, Edwin Forrest, framed by a starfish. The text, by Henry L. Stephens, chides the American public for its adulation of the actor and asks: "What is the summum bonum in this nineteenth century judging by the popular appreciation, and the estimation in which [its] professors are held? Theatrical acquirements!" Stephens caricatured P. T. Barnum as "The Humbug," one of his more inspired characterizations, and included several other contemporary theatrical figures in his attack.

By the early twentieth century, so many publications included drawings that most serious artists of the period began their careers as either sketch artists or caricaturists for newspapers and magazines. It was a way to make a living while they were engaged in more serious pursuits. Styles varied from the simple and economical line drawing in charcoal or pencil to highly detailed and carefully wrought pen-and-ink compositions.

Caricaturists unembarrassedly borrowed techniques from the great masters Doré, Daumier, and Hogarth—and from each other. For many twentieth-century artists, sketching caricatures was something to be dropped as soon as practicable; for others, it became a way of life. Because today periodicals are published in ever-shrinking numbers, only a few newspapers (mostly in New York) include a theatrical caricaturist on the staff, but the art of theatrical caricature will survive as long as Al Hirschfeld and his heirs have life and breath. The theater would be poorer without the body of work left by the caricaturists. They offer us sometimes devastating, oftentimes delightful, always off-center but on-target comments on the theater and its people.

PUCK.

SARAH BERNHARDT, THE MODERN RIZPAH, PROTECTING HER SON FROM THE CLERICAL VULTURES.
[A little Variation on M. Becker's Famous Picture.]

Joseph Keppler, founder of the late nineteenth-century periodical *Puck,* occasionally took pen in hand to comment satirically on the public personae of his day. Here he characterizes Sarah Bernhardt—who was having no easy time of it in the United States on her first tour—as the protector of her bastard son, Maurice, in the face of sharp criticism from the pulpit. The allusion is to the heroine of Alfred Lord Tennyson's poem *Rizpah,* which describes another mother-protector, but the original bearer of the name was an Old Testament figure. (One has to be up on the Bible and *belles lettres* to decipher the cartoons and caricatures that amused our forebears)

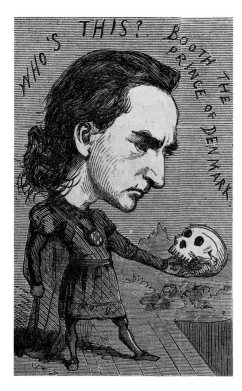

Thomas Nast (1840–1902), greatest of American nineteenth-century caricaturists, sometimes stepped out of politics, his usual arena, to pounce on theatrical personages. His drawing of Edwin Booth as Hamlet, the actor's most famous role, makes light of the famous "Alas, poor Yorick" graveyard scene and of Booth himself. It was published in *Harper's Weekly* on April 5, 1866

Very little is known of W. J. Gladding except that he was assistant in the photographic studio of C. D. Fredericks, one of New York's leading celebrity photographers. In 1868 Gladding drew the caricatures of twelve leading players on the American stage for Colonel T. Allston Brown, editor of the *New York Clipper* and a sometime historian of the American stage. They were assembled and published by the Dunlap Society in 1897. The originals were presented to the Players and are displayed on the walls of the club. They are among the earliest examples of theatrical caricature in American history. In his drawing of Edwin Forrest, one of the first native stars of the American stage, Gladding emphasizes the great actor's bulging biceps and sturdy neck. Forrest was an avid exerciser, a fact attested by the Indian clubs in the background

Carlo de Fornaro (1872–1949) came to America from Italy in 1896 and provided caricatures for *Theatre* magazine, newspapers, and other publications. During a visit to Mexico, he publicly championed the revolutionaries, and at a bizarre trial in 1909, on United States soil, he was convicted of defaming Mexican president Porfirio Diaz and sentenced to a prison term in an American jail! De Fornaro believed that the fewer the lines in a caricature, "the cleverer and wittier it will be." Conciseness is the keynote of this undated study of the beloved American actor Joseph Jefferson. Although Jefferson's career during the last thirty years of his life was dominated by the role of Rip Van Winkle, De Fornaro chose to draw him in formal dress, with a slightly quizzical look on his face

Clare Briggs (1875–1929) was born in Reedsburg, Wisconsin, and his family moved to Lincoln, Nebraska, when he was a boy. He studied at the University of Nebraska, joined a drawing class, and in 1896 journeyed to St. Louis to look for work. He found it as a sketch artist for newspapers in that city, but eventually he moved to New York to further his career. An editor of one of the newspapers for which he freelanced recognized Briggs's comic flair and suggested that he turn his hand to cartoons and caricatures. He took the suggestion and was eventually syndicated by the New York Tribune Company. His undated drawing of George M. Cohan catches the swagger of the great song-and-dance man, renowned on Broadway for his overweening self-confidence

The mentor of many artists at the Art Students League in New York, Boardman Robinson (1876–1962) was by birth a Nova Scotian, the scion of a seafaring family. He studied art at the Massachusetts Normal School and in Paris. From 1907 to 1910, he was on the staff of the *New York Telegraph* and after that of the *New York Tribune*. His swiftly sketched drawings were finished in sepia. Robinson became enmeshed in politics (he accompanied John Reed to Russia) and later abandoned his commercial career to turn to serious painting. His 1910 drawing of Henry Miller and Henry Dixey conveys nothing of the glamour of Broadway stardom. The legendary matinee idols look like portly businessmen, but Dixey had set female hearts aflutter beginning in 1884, when he appeared in tights and makeup as a Greek statue come to life, and Miller had long been a leading man with the famous Empire Theatre stock company

Probably the most prolific American illustrator of his day, James Montgomery Flagg (1877–1960) studied in New York at the Art Students League and in Paris. During his long career, he sketched practically every prominent man and woman in America, and his work appeared in every popular newspaper and magazine. He was a gregarious and affable man, whose circle of acquaintances included many theater luminaries. Although he never ventured into pure caricature, he delighted in adding just a touch of satire to some of his sketches. The great actor John Drew, friend to the artist, was renowned for his good looks and chiseled profile, and this was undoubtedly why in this turn-of-the-century drawing Flagg impishly emphasized the ever-so-slight bump in his nose

"Oh, Lola Pratt! Sweet Lola Pratt!
I Wonder What You're Gazin' At"

The Baby-Talk Lady (Miss Ruth Gordon) and "P'ecious" Seventeen

Ohioan Alfred J. Frueh (1880–1968), "Al Free" of the caricaturists' world, drew for the *St. Louis Post-Dispatch* before making the grand tour in 1909. Back on American soil, he worked for the *New York World* and then in 1925 was hired by Harold Ross as an artist for the *New Yorker,* a post he filled for the rest of his life. During Frueh's fifty-seven-year career, the stars aged with him on paper. His early carica-tures, compiled for a book called *Stage Folk* (1922), were lino-leum cuts, but later he turned to pen-and-ink and pencil. His dev-astating caricature for the *Post-Dispatch* of Fritzi Scheff, who in 1907 was on tour in St. Louis in *Mlle. Modiste,* her perennial ve-hicle, so upset the actress that she cancelled a performance and threatened a lawsuit. Many years later Frueh recalled, "It was very nearly the making of me"

Gluyas Williams (1888–1982) began his career as an artist and illustrator while still an under-graduate, editing the *Harvard Lampoon.* He went to Paris to study art and returned to Boston to work as a caricaturist for the *Boston Journal and Evening Transcript.* Traveling south to New York, he plied his trade for the old *Life* (under Charles Dana Gibson) and eventually became a stalwart of the *New Yorker.* He later teamed up with Harvard classmate Robert Benchley to il-lustrate the humorist's books. Possessed of a superb visual memory, he would observe his subjects and then draw them from his mind's eye. His economy of line is nowhere better shown than in his portrait sketch of actress Ruth Gordon (with pup-py "P'ecious"), who was appear-ing in Boston in Booth Tarkington's *Seventeen,* after the New York run in 1918

A San Franciscan by birth, John Decker (1895–1947) had a brief career as an actor before receiving the call to art. He was a prolific caricaturist and worked steadily for the *New York Evening World* while freelancing for other publications. He wrote: "The sincere caricaturist can have few friends. Only those who are unafraid of truth, who prize reality, can understand him, for his business is to undeceive both his public and his subject. Merely physical exaggeration is nothing, it is necessary that each line should portray the hidden character of the 'victim.'" Decker's victim in this drawing is Lee Shubert, the theater owner who dominated Broadway during the first half of the twentieth century and did not often enjoy a favorable press. Decker did not forget to feature Shubert's sartorial splendor, persistent five-o'clock shadow, and self-satisfied expression, as he pictured him going about his business, hands in pockets, renting theaters

William Auerbach-Levy (1889–1964) made New York City his exclusive turf, and he ventured away only to study art in Paris, after attending City College and the National Academy of Design. He had a talent for etching and taught it—art and process—at the National Academy School of Fine Arts on his return. Attracted to the art of caricature, he submitted a sample to a contest sponsored by the Pennsylvania Academy of the Fine Arts and won the prize. That accolade launched him on a new career. In 1925 he was hired as carica- turist by the *New York World,* and during his lifetime he turned out thousands of caricatures for the *New York Post,* the *Brooklyn Eagle,* the *New Yorker, Vanity Fair, Vogue,* and many other magazines and newspapers. His book of caricatures, *Is That Me?* (1947), presents a broad spectrum of his work. In 1922 John Barrymore was garnering triumphant critical notices for his portrayal of Hamlet on Broadway, but Auerbach-Levy's sly caricature was not a rave for his spindly legs

Reginald Marsh (1898–1954) began drawing cartoons for the *Yale Record.* After leaving the university, Marsh received assignments from *Vanity Fair* and *Harper's Bazaar,* but his first important job was as caricaturist for the *New York Daily News.* There, from 1922 to 1925, he produced drawings he called "cartoonicles," in which he rated theatrical and vaudeville performers on a percentage basis. Eventually, he abandoned his commercial career (he also sketched for the *New Yorker, Esquire, Life,* and *Fortune*) and turned to painting, becoming associated with John Sloan and the Art Students League. Marsh's caricatures are as vividly detailed as his later paintings and they draw heavily on the seamier side of theatrical life. The cartoonicles illustrated here reveal his predilection for vaudeville in the 1920s. Al Jolson he rates at 100 percent, while poor Fritzi Scheff comes in at a mere 20 percent

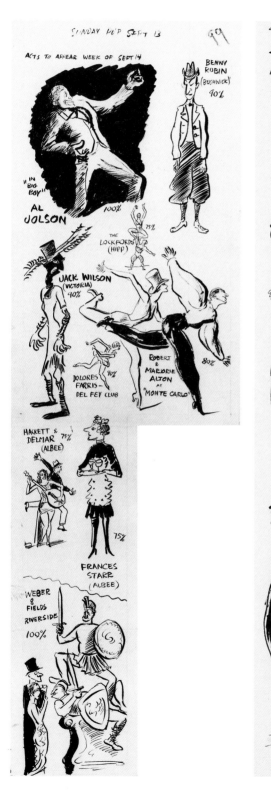

Abe Birnbaum (1898-1966), a Manhattanite by birth, studied at the Art Students League under Boardman Robinson. During his lifetime, he contributed more drawings and cartoons to the *New Yorker* than any other artist. In addition, his work was published in *Harper's Bazaar, Vogue,* and such New York newspapers as the *Herald Tribune, World, Post,* and *Telegram.* A painstaking draftsman, he would labor long and hard over a drawing to achieve the greatest effect with boldness and simplicity of line. Caricaturists leave no star unstoned, no matter how beloved they may be. One of Helen Hayes's greatest triumphs was in J. M. Barrie's *What Every Woman Knows,* but Birnbaum's 1926 study of her in the role of Maggie is less than flattering

Charm and Quietude.

Helen Hayes

Above:

Peggy Bacon (1895–1987) was the daughter of artists and studied at the Art Students League under John Sloan, George Bellows, and Max Weber. She enjoyed a long career as a caricaturist, illustrator, and author. She was called the Dorothy Parker of ink and crayon because her caricatures frequently went straight to the jugular vein of her subjects. She published a number of books, among which was *Off with Their Heads!* (1934), a collection of trenchant caricatures of notable people in the arts. Her work also appeared in the *New Yorker,* the *Delineator,* and the *Theatre Guild Bulletin.* Shown is her impression of George Gershwin, whom she described as having a "shoe-box" head and "flat cheeks, ironed out, sweeping aggressively into bulging lip and chin"

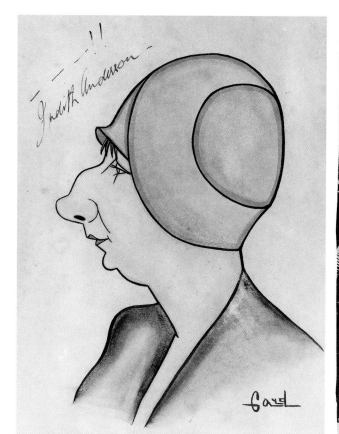

The Good Bad Showman

Alex Gard (1900–1948) came to the United States in 1924 via Paris and other way stations. His drawings began to appear weekly in the *New York Herald Tribune*'s drama section, but he is probably best remembered as the first official caricaturist for Sardi's, the leading theatrical spa in New York. Many of his drawings still grace (if that is the word) the walls of the restaurant, whose owner gave Gard free meals for his efforts. Gard's caricatures of the stars were generally corrosive, as this undated example picturing Judith Anderson will testify, but celebrities were always delighted to land on Sardi's walls, no matter how unflattering the likeness

Miguel Covarrubias (1904–1957) arrived in New York from Mexico on an art scholarship in 1922 and was assisted early in his career by H. L. Mencken and Carl Van Vechten. He skipped the usual apprenticeship of drawing for the dailies and went to work immediately for Frank Crowninshield of *Vanity Fair* and later for Harold Ross of the *New Yorker*. His work was also published in *New York World, Life, Time, Fortune, McCall's, Holiday*, and other popular magazines. A man of exceptional talent, Covarrubias turned to painting and eventually went back to Mexico, where he received a number of commissions to paint murals in public buildings. Many caricaturists, including Al Hirschfeld, feel that they

owe him a debt for raising the standards of caricature drawing and honing it into an art. In this undated drawing Covarrubias depicts David Belasco, legendary producer of the early twentieth century. Belasco was the stuff of caricature, and he often appeared in some sort of transfiguration in the press of his time. A notorious Broadway playboy, he nonetheless affected clerical garb for reasons known only to him. (Belasco mentioned a priest who had taught him as a child, but there was much that was fictional in the account of his early life.) Disingenuously sad of face, he greets two ladies in Times Square, the happy hunting ground for his conquests. Note the caption

Opposite:

In this drawing of Fanny Brice in *Fanny* (1926), a vehicle for her own special talents written by David Belasco and Willard Mack, Covarrubias creates a face that is Picassoesque (note the eyes) and conveys an energy through curved lines juxtaposed against hard lines and sharp angles. No wonder the next generation of caricaturists chose him as a model

Born in 1917 in New York, Sam Norkin, at the age of nine was placed in a special art class that his older brother was also attending. He continued art studies at the Brooklyn Museum Art School and Cooper Union (among other institutions) and aspired to become a poster designer. His first job diverted his career into caricaturing. While working in the art department of the *New York Herald Tribune,* he occasionally saw one of his drawings published in the theater pages. In 1956 he was hired by the *New York Daily News* as the paper's full-time caricaturist and he remained there until his recent retirement. During his tenure, he handled all assignments in the theater, opera, dance, and film. Norkin was one of the first major New York caricaturists to have his drawings scooped up by press agents and sent to out-of-town newspapers. In this drawing, dated December 11, 1949, he shows the road company of Tennessee Williams's *Streetcar Named Desire* all aboard for the tour throughout the country

Opposite:

Irving Hoffman (1909–1968) began his career as a caricaturist at the age of fourteen, when he attended the 1924 Democratic National Convention in New York. There he sketched William Jennings Bryan, Al Smith, and Franklin Delano Roosevelt and promptly sold the drawings to the *New York Evening World.* From that point on, he put education behind him, entering the newspaper world first as caricaturist for the *New York Morning Telegraph* and later as columnist for the *Holly-wood Reporter.* In between those assignments, he freelanced as a Broadway press agent, writer, and caricaturist. Although his favorite subject was himself, he drew hundreds of caricatures of Broadway and Hollywood stars. Hoffman's gloriously stylized rendering of Mae West (appearing in *Diamond Lil* in 1928) does not fail to emphasize her most conspicuous feature: the famous hourglass figure. This drawing appeared in *Theatre Magazine,* September 1928

Caricature by IRVING HOFFMANN

"DIAMOND LIL" HERSELF

Mae West—Interpreter of Rip-Roaring Melodrama

She flared into notoriety when her indelicate opus, SEX, was suppressed last year, and she was sent on a short holiday to the local government's retreat for civic sinners. She has "come back" with a whoopee in DIAMOND LIL, her play of New York's old-time underworld.

The artistic career of Irma Selz (1908–1975) started with her work on the University of Chicago newspaper. In 1932, she moved to New York, like many of her colleagues, to earn fame and fortune. Gradually, she began to receive assignments from *Vanity Fair, Harper's Bazaar,* and the New York dailies. She went to work full time for the *New York Post* during the McCarthy era and produced many caricatures of the political figures at center stage. Her caricature of Picasso was acquired by the Tate Gallery, in London. Selz enjoyed the theater and theatrical caricaturing. She worked from life in pencil, later finishing the drawings in pen and ink at home. In this backstage drawing made during the run of *Star and Garter* in 1942, Selz makes light of Gypsy Rose Lee fulfilling her dual career as author and performer

Opposite:

Acknowledged today as the dean of theatrical caricaturists, the peerless artist of the simple line, Albert Hirschfeld was born in 1903 in St. Louis. He planned to become a painter and sculptor and, after study in New York, he settled in Paris in 1924 to develop his talents in both arts, but succumbed in the end to his fascination with the manipulation of line with pen and pencil. His early drawings were submitted to the *New York World* and the *New York Tribune,* but from 1925 to the present he has worked exclusively for the *New York Times.* As caricaturist for the *Times,* he has attracted a worldwide following and has a gallery in New York that deals exclusively with his work. His warm friend and col-

league the late *Times* drama critic Brooks Atkinson once defined Hirschfeld's technique as "not so much distortions of fact as enlargements of the total personality. Although his drawings are fantastifications, they are from the inside out. Instead of burlesquing people, he joins them on their own terms, adding his own gaiety for good measure." For many years, Hirschfeld has woven the name of his daughter Nina into the tapestry of his drawings, and if he decides to include it more than once, he has taken to slipping a small numeral next to his signature to indicate the exact number

Before Al Hirschfeld developed the expressive line that is so much a part of his work for the *New York Times,* he tried other artistic modes—for exam-

ple, a pointillist, somewhat Beardsley-esque style. Subject of this 1928 pen-and-ink sketch is Florence Reed as the celebrated brothel-owner in *The Shanghai Gesture,* originally produced on Broadway in 1926 and revived two years later

One of Al Hirschfeld's more in-spired flights of fancy was his creation of caricatures depicting improbable castings of plays. Here shown are Ethel Merman and Ernest Borgnine, Hirsch-feld's 1964 pick for Noel Cow-ard's *Private Lives.* It is a double-edged satire on the brief-est of marriages between this couple mismatched in real life and in the play

There are three *Nina*s in Al Hirschfeld's rendition of two of America's leading playwrights, Tennessee Williams and Arthur Miller, a study of sophistication on the one hand and a profes-sorial and earnest casualness on the other. The caricaturist al-ways knows how to capture essences

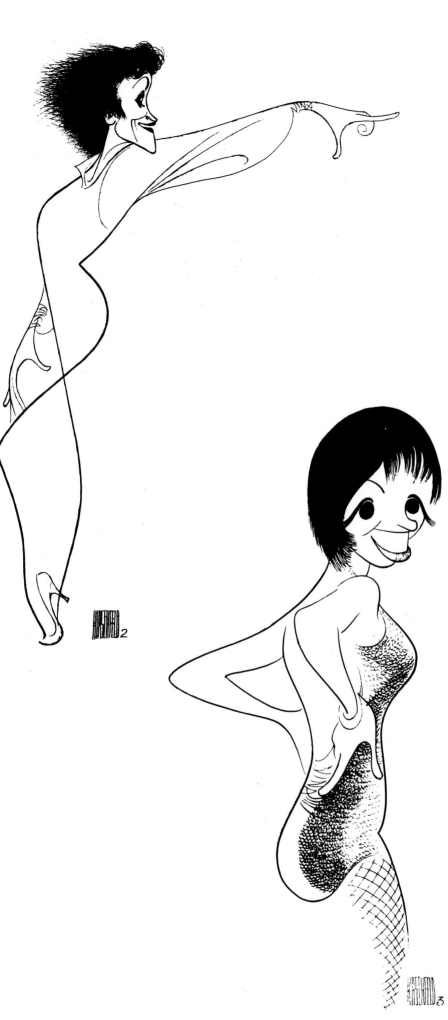

Al Hirschfeld's marvelous economy of line is nowhere better illustrated than in this caricature of Chita Rivera (March 2, 1984). The dancer's body and energy are displayed with one seamless stroke of the pen. To enjoy a Hirschfeld caricature with any regularity these days, one must consult the Broadway column in the Friday *New York Times*

Time was when an Al Hirschfeld caricature always adorned the front pages of the "Arts and Leisure" section of the *New York Times* Sunday edition. The steady decline of the theater in America is underscored by this small fact: today, only infrequently does a Hirschfeld caricature appear on any page of the Sunday newspapers. On October 23, 1977, Hirschfeld supplied the *Times* with this delightfully malicious drawing of Liza Minnelli, who was about to sweep into town in *The Act,* an entertainment hand-tailored to her talents

Programs

The American theater program is unique in that it is almost always given away free to ticket holders (in England and abroad it is almost always sold to the audience by the ushers). During the past two hundred years, it has evolved into something akin to a magazine, including within its pages information about fashions, wining and dining, and theatrical figures or celebrities, along with a smorgasbord of advertisements, many in color. Finally, it defies extinction. In any average American middle-class home, piled next to the *National Geographic* magazines can be found neatly tied bundles of theater programs. That these ephemeral treasures survive the occasion they once served is surely a testament to the collecting instinct that afflicts a sizable portion of humanity, and also, perhaps, to some elusive, indestructible quality of their own. Whatever the reasons, they have become documents of the history of the theater, and it is safe to say that the larger history of civilization would be incomplete and duller without them.

Since American theater is rooted in English theater, it is across the Atlantic that we must go to discover the origin of the American program, programme or playbill, by all of which names it has been known. For years, theater historians have been searching for the oldest example in the English language, and the quest has not stopped. In 1952 an English scholar found one dated 1672 among the papers of Charles II, the first of the Restoration kings. Bearing the royal coat of arms as an expression of official approval, this playbill for an outdoor booth theater at Charing Cross gives the time and date of a performance and a smattering of information about what is to be presented. Without mentioning the cast, it merely states that the play will be acted "by Men and Women." It measures nine by seven inches and was probably used both as a handout at the performance and as a poster.

Certainly one of the most colorful of the theatrical souvenir
books was designed by scenic
artist Sergei Soudeikine for
Nikita Balieff's revue *Chauve-
Souris,* a potpourri of Russian
vaudeville-type entertainment,
consisting of folk songs and
dances and comic skits, that
made its appearance and reap-
pearance in America in 1922,
1925, 1927, and 1929

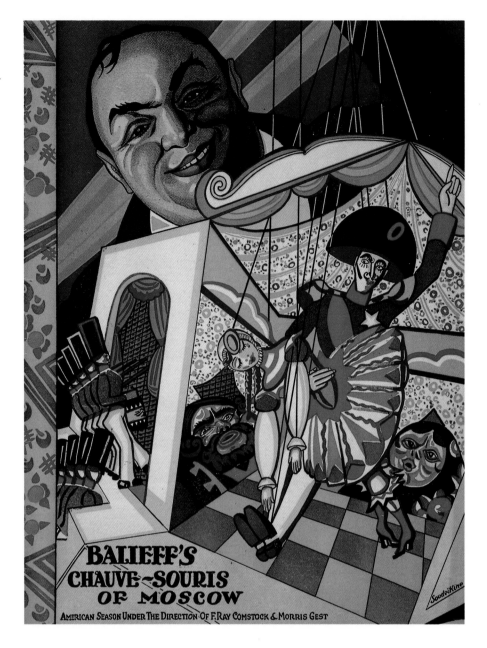

By the beginning of the eighteenth century, playbills provided more details about a
performance, including a list of the actors and the parts they were playing. They also began to be
sold within the theaters, at first by the pert orange-sellers and then by the married women or
the "stock old maids" in the acting companies. Outside the playhouses, street urchins hawked
them for a penny.

The early English playbills looked like title pages for books. Because existing typefaces were
few, the printers could vary the playbills chiefly by changing the spacing and borders or by
setting the titles and important information in capitals. Since it had not yet dawned upon actors
that the playbills could boost their careers as well as their egos, the early specimens are
models of restraint. The names of the cast are given in order of the importance of the characters'
status in the play (thus, King Duncan, a bit part in *Macbeth,* preceded Macbeth, the leading
role), but the ladies' names *always* trailed the men's. It was David Garrick, the greatest English
actor of the mid-to-late eighteenth century, who recognized the publicity potential of the playbill

ZIEGFELD ROOF
Atop New Amsterdam Theatre

A Ziegfeld Beauty
DRAWN BY
- RAPHAEL -
- KIRCHNER -

Ziegfeld Midnight Frolic

COPYRIGHTED NEW YORK THEATRE PROGRAM CORPORATION

"An Ancient Prejudice has been Removed"

LUCKY STRIKE "IT'S TOASTED" **CIGARETTES**

Because -
Toasting takes
out that bite
and throat
irritation

"It's toasted"
<u>No Throat Irritation–No Cough.</u>

The program of about 1915 shown at left features a winsome chorus girl from Flo Ziegfeld's *Midnight Frolic,* an after-show, roof-garden entertainment that served as a showcase for untried performers and ideas in germination for mainstage revues at Ziegfeld's New Amsterdam Theatre. At that date, the beauty's lighted cigarette would have been a daring touch. By 1929, the date of the program advertisement for Lucky Strikes (above), cigarette companies were advertising as frequently in theater programs as they are today. Pictured is another Ziegfeld beauty. Although the ad proclaims "an ancient prejudice has been removed," the name of the showgirl (Myrna Darby, one of the last of the Ziegfeld girls) was discreetly blacked out after publication, indicating that American women had not yet come a very long way

In the early years of the twentieth century, when a theater's program became its signature, cover designs were colorful, fanciful, and distinctive. On this page and pages 157–59 is a selection of program covers from about 1906 to the 1920s—nine for New York theaters, the others for playhouses in Chicago and Boston. The Comedy Theatre cover (right), copyrighted in 1906, was still in use when the avant-garde Washington Square Players leased the house for their productions in 1917

Right:

Program cover, Comedy Theatre, New York, c. 1906

Program cover, Wallack's Theatre, New York, c. 1906

Below:

Program cover, Gaiety Theatre, New York, c. 1908

Program cover, Weber's Theatre, New York, c. 1910

Comedy Theatre
The Washington Square Players

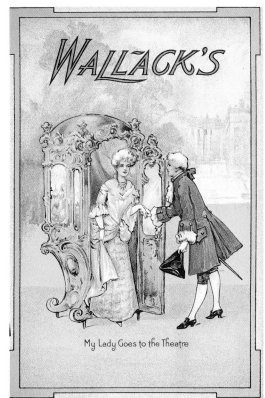

WALLACK'S

My Lady Goes to the Theatre

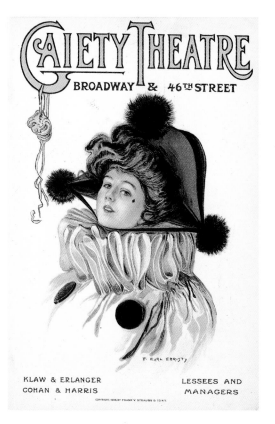

GAIETY THEATRE
BROADWAY & 46TH STREET

KLAW & ERLANGER
COHAN & HARRIS

LESSEES AND
MANAGERS

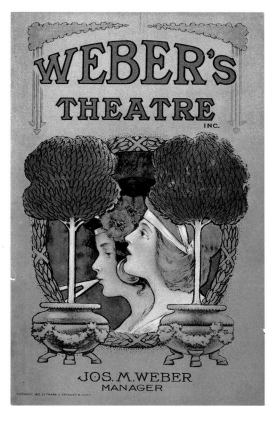

WEBER'S THEATRE
INC.

JOS. M. WEBER
MANAGER

Program cover, Sam S. Shubert
Theatre, New York, n.d.

Program cover, A. H. Woods
Theatre, Chicago, c. 1920s

Right:

Program cover, Casino Theatre, New York, c. 1914

Below:

Program cover designed for the Orpheum Co., New York, c. 1911

Program cover, Bronx Opera House, c. 1921

Program cover, Majestic Theatre, Boston, 1922

Opposite:

Program cover, Fulton Theatre, New York, c. 1921

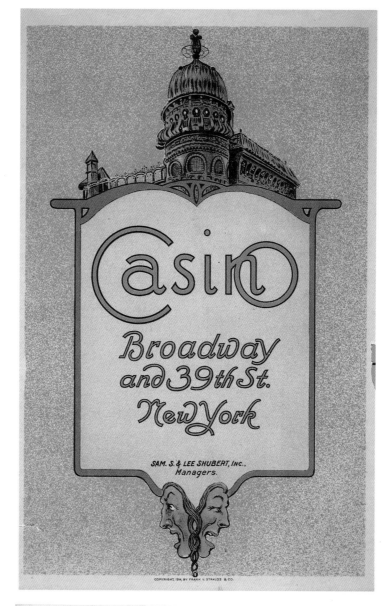

FULTON
THEATRE
46TH ST. WEST OF BROADWAY

OLIVER D. BAILEY
SOLE LESSEE AND MANAGER

Program cover, Selwyn Theatre,
New York, c. 1922

Color returned to the *Playbill* cover in 1961, with the opening night program for *Kean,* a play that starred Alfred Drake as the great English tragedian, but it was not until *Baker Street* (1965) that a color cover was used for the full run of a show. Because it is so expensive, only the most optimistic of producers will order his covers in color and insisted that his name be printed in large letters in the center of the sheet. Within a short time, all of the great stars of the London stage were demanding prominent positions on the playbills. The managers, musicians, and stage designers soon also clamored for space, pushing the program into larger and larger formats.

It was about this time in history that English actors made their first appearance on American shores. They traveled along the eastern seaboard (but not into New England) in troupes that more nearly resembled bands of English provincial players than the great London companies. If they printed programs, a doubtful hypothesis, none has survived from the first half of the eighteenth century. The earliest American playbill was preserved through providential accident. It was pasted on the wooden back of an old mirror, probably as a filler, and was later varnished for protection. Eventually, it came into the hands of an avid collector, Evert Jansen Wendell, who bequeathed his entire hoard to the Harvard Theatre Collection. The program is dated March 27, 1750, and, although much of it is obliterated, we can still see that a performance of *The Orphan* was to be followed by a farce, *The Beau in the Sudds,* at the Theatre in Nassau Street, New York City. A newspaper advertisement for the performance supplies the missing information: the price of the seats was five shillings for the "pitt" (today's orchestra) and three for the "gallery" (balcony), with the performance to begin "precisely at half an Hour after 6 o'Clock." The names of the cast were not included.

Later American playbills reflect the terse format of English programs but sometimes unintentionally provide tantalizing bits of additional information. For instance, when the first important troupe of British actors came to the colonies, in 1752, they billed themselves as the London Company of Comedians, but in 1763, with the tide of revolutionary spirit rising in America, the troupe's manager, David Douglass, changed its name to the American Company of Comedians. Prerevolutionary playbills almost invariably ended the list of credits with the phrase "Vivat Rex" (Long Live the King), but when the troupe ventured back to the United States of America, the phrase was changed to "Vivat Republica."

These early thespians learned the hard way to step warily through the political thickets of the New World. The conservative precincts of New England were notoriously difficult to breach. Even the tactful and resourceful David Douglass could get no farther north than Providence, Rhode Island, and then only by dint of recasting his repertoire of plays as a series of "Moral Dialogues." To what lengths he had to go can be deduced from a playbill of August 25, 1762, for a performance of *The Provok'd Husband,* a once-rousing Restoration comedy by Sir John Vanbrugh, modified to expose "for the edification of New England," as the program cannily puts it, "the evils of unbridled ambition that is not Supported by Moral Purpose and the Unfortunate Results of Wifely Disobedience of a Wife and Indulgent Spouse."

The nineteenth century brought many changes in the American theater program. The number of typefaces available to the printer had increased enormously. He was able to employ fat, tall, small, thin and decorative letters, in roman and italic styles, and sometimes he combined them all in one playbill. Frequently, the program became a hodgepodge of the printer's art. Because of the vagaries of the early presses (powered first by man, then by steam) ink was

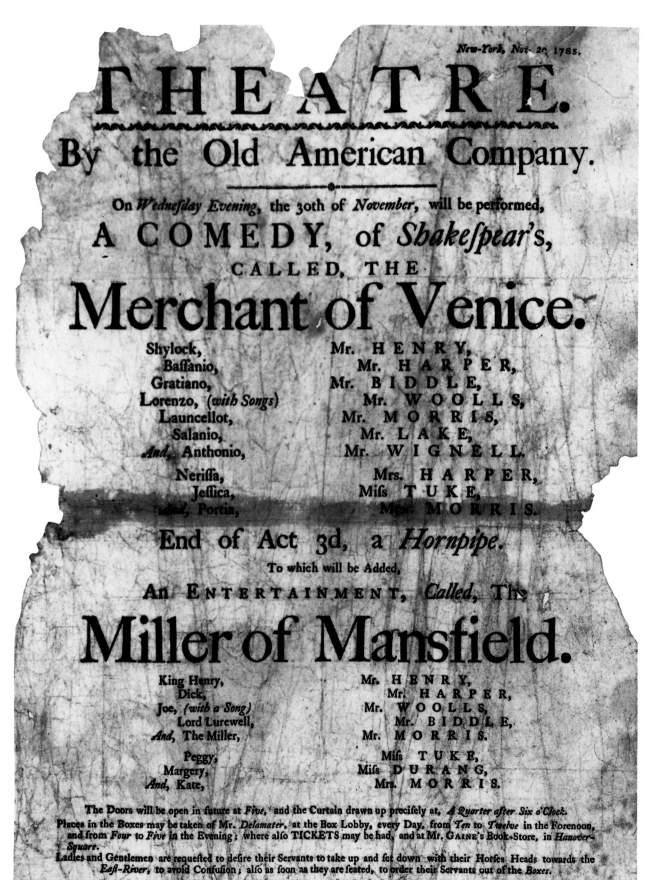

New-York, Nov. 20, 1785.

THEATRE.

By the Old American Company.

On *Wednesday Evening*, the 30th of *November*, will be performed,

A COMEDY, of *Shakespear's*,

CALLED, THE

Merchant of Venice.

Shylock,	Mr. HENRY,
Baſſanio,	Mr. HARPER,
Gratiano,	Mr. BIDDLE,
Lorenzo, (*with Songs*)	Mr. WOOLLS,
Launcellot,	Mr. MORRIS,
Salanio,	Mr. LAKE,
And, Anthonio,	Mr. WIGNELL.
Neriſſa,	Mrs. HARPER,
Jeſſica,	Miſs TUKE,
And, Portia,	Mrs. MORRIS.

End of Act 3d, a *Hornpipe*.

To which will be Added,

An ENTERTAINMENT, *Called*, The

Miller of Mansfield.

King Henry,	Mr. HENRY,
Dick,	Mr. HARPER,
Joe, (*with a Song*)	Mr. WOOLLS,
Lord Lurewell,	Mr. BIDDLE,
And, The Miller,	Mr. MORRIS.
Peggy,	Miſs TUKE,
Margery,	Miſs DURANG,
And, Kate,	Mrs. MORRIS.

The Doors will be open in future at *Five*, and the Curtain drawn up precisely at, *A Quarter after Six o'Clock.*

Places in the Boxes may be taken of Mr. *Delamater*, at the Box Lobby, every Day, from *Ten* to *Twelve* in the Forenoon, and from *Four* to *Five* in the Evening; where alſo TICKETS may be had, and at Mr. GAINE's Book-Store, in *Hanover-Square.*

Ladies and Gentlemen are requeſted to deſire their Servants to take up and ſet down with their Horſes Heads towards the *Eaſt-River*, to avoid Confuſion; alſo as ſoon as they are ſeated, to order their Servants out of the *Boxes.*

BOX 8s. PIT 6s. and GALLERY 4s.

⁂ *No Perſon to be admitted behind the Scenes, on any Account whatever.*

The Public are reſpectfully informed, the Days of Performance will be, *Mondays, Wedneſdays and Fridays.*

Vivat Reſpublica.

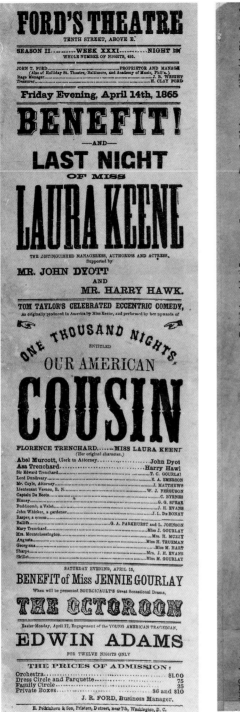

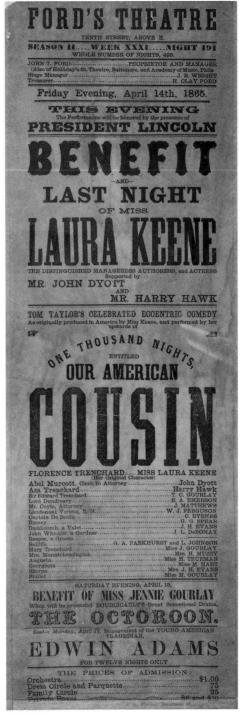

On Friday evening, April 14, 1865, almost on the spur of the moment, President Abraham Lincoln attended a production of *Our American Cousin* at Ford's Theatre in Washington, D.C., and there he was assassinated. The original handbill for the performance is shown at left. The version at right is the creation of L. Brown, who like other printers seized the main chance and issued fake handbills with the name of the dead president prominently displayed. Sold as the genuine article (some of the fakes even had spots of the president's "blood" on them), the counterfeit had wider currency than the real one—even though the printer of the original bill eventually joined the scramble by reprinting his program for extra profit. Today, only an expert can distinguish the fakes from the real programs

Opposite:

After the Revolution, the American Company of Comedians, which had sat out the war on the island of Jamaica, made its way back to New York and reopened the old John Street Theatre. The first season began in November 1785 and, as this handbill announces, the troupe performed *The Merchant of Venice,* followed by an afterpiece, *The Miller of Mansfield.* This small, single sheet had to serve many purposes: it was a program, a handout, and a poster. It gives all the pertinent information—date, cast, curtain time, prices, and the days of performance—and represents an advance over the sketchy documents of prior times

SOUVENIR·ALBUM

SCENES OF THE PLAY.

BEN·HUR

COPYRIGHTED, 1900, BY KLAW & ERLANGER.

AMERICAN COLORTYPE CO., N. Y. & CHI.

Ever eager to turn a new profit, producers Marc Klaw and Abraham Erlanger printed and sold a souvenir book for their production of the evergreen *Ben Hur* (1899). It included a series of reproductions of Joseph Byron photographs of the spectacle. Seen here is the cover, with an illustration—Classical in flavor—of the famous chariot race

WILLIAM A. BRADY'S

PLAYHOUSE

Forty-eighth Street, East of Broadway

Monday Evening, May 20, 1912

WILLIAM A. BRADY (Ltd.)

Presents for the

300th Performance in New York

"Bought and Paid For"

A Play in Four Acts

By GEORGE BROADHURST

CAST

Robert Stafford.........................Charles Richman
James Gilley.............................Frank Craven
Oku.......................................Allen Atwell
Louis.....................................Edgar Hill
Virginia Blaine...........................Julia Dean
Fanny Blaine.............................Marie Nordstrom
Josephine................................Dorothy Davies

SYNOPSIS

Act I—Robert Stafford's Apartments
Act II—Mrs. Stafford's Boudoir (two years later)
Act III—Same as Act II (the next morning)
Act IV—James Gilley's Flat (nearly three months later)

Place: New York City   Time: The Present

Production under the stage direction of Edward Elsner
Scenery built by Burt Tucman Painted by H. Robert Law

Souvenir programs are a way of advertising success. In more affluent times, a producer would frequently print a program on colored silk or satin for distribution to the audience at a landmark performance. In this case, William A. Brady heralded the three-hundredth performance of *Bought and Paid For* on May 20, 1912, in a pale blue satin handout showing his theater and the marquee

Neither a program nor a souvenir book, a herald is an advertising piece that made its serious debut in the 1920s. Letter-size, it can be left on hotel desks or ticket-brokers' counters or folded and mailed to subscribers to theater-ticket clubs. Sometimes it bears the same image as the show's poster, and sometimes it is redesigned into something that looks quite different. Always the herald appears after a show has hit its stride because it includes comments by reviewers. Here and opposite are three photographs of the herald for *Desire under the Elms* (1924), closed and open. As a play made the rounds of the country, the herald was altered by the simple insertion of the name of each local theater and the dates of each local run

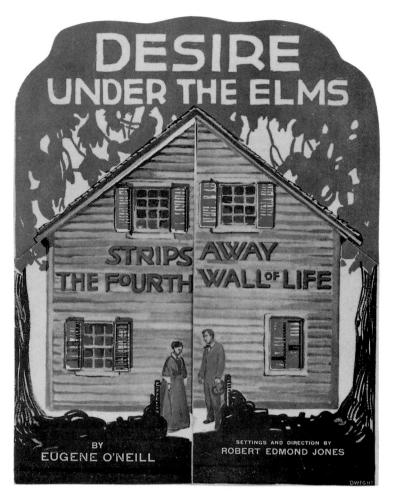

applied heavily or lightly, but hardly ever consistently. Complaints were many and frequent as gloves became soiled by ink-soaked programs—or when the printing was barely legible. The playbill was designed, if that is the word, in the composing room by job or commercial printers, usually subsidiaries of newspaper plants. The paper was often similar in quality to newsprint and has proved to be a challenge for conservators trying to preserve it for the centuries.

When theater became established in the cultural life of the nation in the nineteenth century, the program became an advertisement. The managers used it to extol themselves, their stars, new scenery and costumes, and the play itself. Hyperbole was the order of the day (and it still is). A synopsis of the play might be printed in almost illegible small type, previews of coming attractions might be included, and, by mid-century, line drawings of the stars or spectacular scenes from the play were added as an inducement to theatergoers. Billing of the performers became a no-man's-land of actor-manager combat. The greater the star, the larger his name appeared on the playbill, until the billing dwarfed the title of the play. Today, a star's contract will specify in precise detail the position of his or her name in the program and the size and style of type relative to all other names. Many a tense moment in agents' offices has been spent resolving the issue of billing.

The long, thin playbills of the first half of the nineteenth century were displaced in the late nineteenth century by smaller, folded, pamphlet-like programs. By the 1870s, many of the elegant first-class playhouses published their own programs; other theaters were provided with

DESIRE UNDER THE ELMS

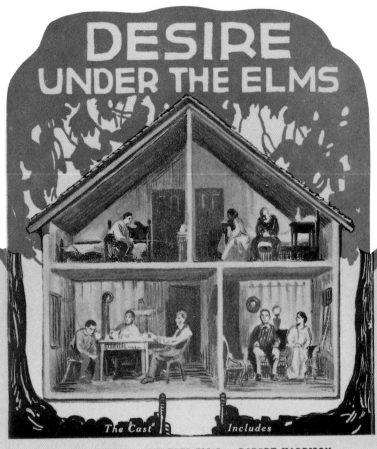

MARY MORRIS · CHARLES ELLIS · ROBERT HARRISON

The Cast Includes

"Eugene O'Neill has given us a powerful play, straightforward like nature, and almost as inevitable in its sequence. While the episode has tragedy and daring, it is far too sincere and sombre to be salacious; rather does it approach the fateful march of the Greek tragedies. It renders high service to the cause of art and to the public."
Dr. S. E. Mezes,
Pres. College of the City of New York.

"A Master work of its kind. The production and the playing are profoundly impressive. Every student of the theatre and American plays should see it."
Burns Mantle in N. Y. Daily News.

"Hewn from the stuff of life itself. Marked from first to last with boldness and imagination."
Alexander Woollcott in N.Y. Sun.

"Mature conception. Imaginative austerity. Setting profoundly dramatic. Such poetry and terrible beauty as we seldom see in the theatre."
Stark Young in New York Times.

"'Desire Under The Elms' is a tragedy, a real tragedy, with the power, starkness and nobility which only real tragedy can assume. I only ask to be shown anything produced by the English-speaking theatre of recent generations which is half so fine or true or brave as 'Desire Under The Elms'."
Sidney Howard — Author of
"They Knew What They Wanted"

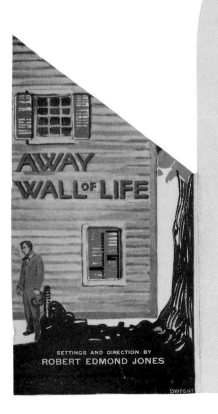

AWAY
WALL OF LIFE

SETTINGS AND DIRECTION BY
ROBERT EDMOND JONES

EUGENE O'NEILL'S "Desire Under The Elms" is the most talked about play of our generation. By many critics, lay and professional alike, it is judged the finest play yet written by an American. Its austere realism, its graphic and bitter portrayal of man at grips with nature, has caused it to be compared favorably with the Greek tragedies.

The story of "Desire Under The Elms" is the story of man's struggle with his environment. Specifically it is the story of Ephraim Cabot, 70, hard and stern New Englander, his struggles with the rocky and relentless soil and his heroic clashes with life, love and his God. The setting is a New England farm house; the time, 1850.

The popularity of "Desire Under The Elms" has already surpassed that of any tragedy ever played in this country. The company which will play "Desire Under The Elms" in this city is the same company, with a single exception, that appeared in the play for 45 weeks in New York, a run without parallel in our theatre for a play of this type.

"Desire Under The Elms" has won the vigorous endorsement of men in all walks of professional and artistic life. Among those who have applauded its merit and distinction are:

Norman Hapgood, Edward Sheldon, Walter Pritchard Eaton, John Farrar, Joseph Urban, Richard Bennett, George Jean Nathan, Percy Mackaye, Don Marquis, Will Irwin, Frederick Macmonnies, Edward Knobloch, Ring Lardner, Dorothy Gish, John Corbin, Augustus Thomas, Herbert Bayard Swope, John Haynes Holmes, Inez Hayes Irwin, and Ralph Block.

VICTORY THEATRE
DAYTON, OHIO
2 NIGHTS BEGIN. TUES., NOVEMBER 24
POPULAR WEDNESDAY MATINEE

GOLDEN PTG. SERVICE, N. Y.

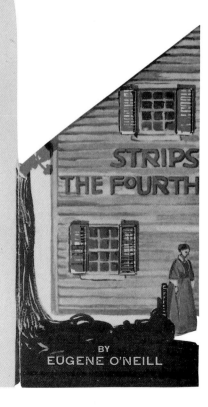

STRIPS
THE FOURTH

BY
EUGENE O'NEILL

BLOSSOM TIME

all-purpose playbills printed under the title *The Stage* or *The Season*. These carried a multitude of small and large ads that all but smothered the information (filled in by the theater) about the play and the cast, but because of the advertising revenues they generated, they could be ordered and distributed free of charge.

The new magazine-style programs were strewn with fillers: jokes, puns, bits of theatrical lore, and household hints. The covers became more and more decorative, colored paper and inks were introduced, and the longer roster of names included everyone but the cloakroom attendants. The ads hawked everything from A to Z. In a program of 1891, for example, a line drawing of a corset resembling a medieval instrument of torture was accompanied by the statement that it had won a gold medal in the Paris Exposition of 1889. And about this time the stars, too, began to lend their endorsements to a variety of products.

In 1866 the principle of the "hit" show became established with *The Black Crook*, which held the boards in New York for sixteen months. The playbill for that long-running and highly profitable production begat fanciful variations in the form of special souvenir programs and set a precedent for future hits. Most of the subsequent souvenir programs were printed on colored silk or satin, some with tassels, to commemorate the landmark performances. (One of the most

Souvenir programs can be used as a guide to American musical styles—and as a gauge of the price of a ticket to the show. Produced by the brothers Shubert in 1921, *Blossom Time* (a musical based loosely on the life of Franz Schubert, which proved to be a perennial favorite with audiences and a big money-earner for the producers) was revived again and again. Anyone could have a permanent record of it, in the form of a souvenir book, for twenty-five cents (opposite). David Merrick's souvenir book for *42nd Street* (1980)—in bold red and featuring a fetching, scantily clad chorine (left)—cost a lot more but contained roughly the same ingredients as its demure predecessor unusual specimens was printed on a sheet of aluminum for the Alvin Theater in Pittsburgh.) Early souvenir programs were given away free, usually on the anniversaries of the run (100, 200, 1,000 performances); but later, producers capitalized on the popularity of their plays and players by charging a modest fee. The tradition continues today for the spectacular musicals, but the modest fee has escalated to five dollars or more.

In 1884 a young man from Ohio, Frank V. Strauss, secured the right to gather advertising for the programs of the Madison Square Theatre, which was fast becoming the most prestigious playhouse in New York. Within a few years, Strauss became not only the theater's advertising agent but the publisher of its programs, thereby founding the company that to this day does business in New York under the registered name of *Playbill,* the nation's largest producer of theater programs.

Having merged with his only competitor in 1891, Strauss began supplying programs to New York and out-of-town theaters, for which privilege he paid the owner or manager a small stipend. Though he individualized the covers, at the same time he standardized the form, the quality of paper, and the typeface, and his product became the model for programs published in the major theater centers in the United States. In 1918—having discarded his Germanic-sounding surname during World War I—Frank Storrs (né Strauss) sold his company to his nephew, who made further changes in the program and in 1934 officially registered the New York program as *The Playbill* so that no other company in the country could publish under that name.

Programs today tend to look the same no matter who produces them and under what name. They are laden with advertisements (which pay their way) and include general-interest features for those with a few minutes to spare before, during, and after the performance. Rarely are they left behind. Eventually, many are bundled up and offered to libraries and museums. The ultimate compliment to the American theater program was probably paid by the critic Gilbert Gabriel, who, in reviewing a play not worth his attention, commented, "They should have played the program notes instead of the script."

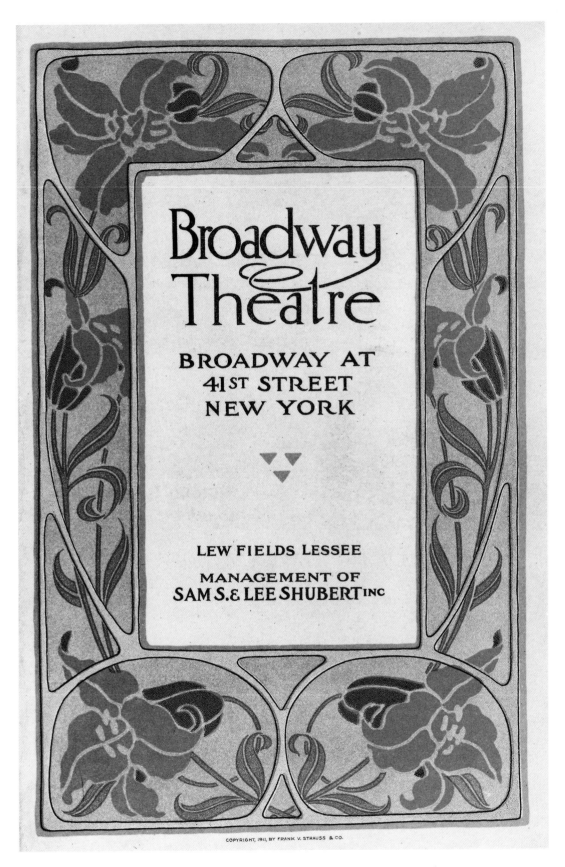

Beginning about 1910, an individualized cover was designed for each theater by the New York printing company that supplied the programs for most of the Broadway houses. In 1930, the type of colorful cover that adorns the program for the Broadway Theatre seen at left was replaced by generic playbills printed in sepia ink on beige backgrounds, usually featuring a print or engraving of a scene from past theater history. In 1934, the program was officially registered as *The Playbill* and, with the omission of the article, so it has remained. Thereafter, theater programs began to advertise the name of the show on the front cover and, after some experimentation with the masthead, they are now instantly recognizable by a bright yellow band across the top. On this page and pages 172–75 is a selection of typical covers from 1911 to 1989

Program cover for the Broadway Theatre, New York, 1911

THE PLAYBILL

WINTER GARDEN

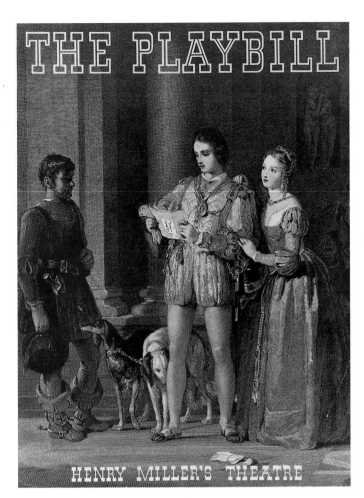

THE PLAYBILL

HENRY MILLER'S THEATRE

The PLAYBILL for The Imperial Theatre

CALL ME MADAM

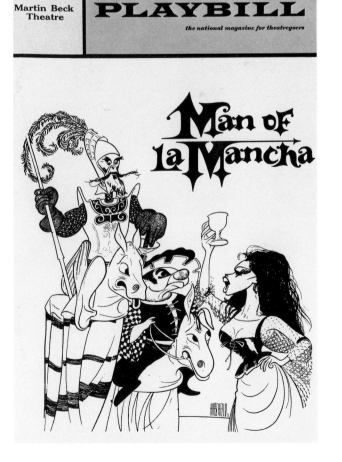

Martin Beck Theatre | PLAYBILL
the national magazine for theatregoers

Man of La Mancha

Opposite:

Program cover for the Winter Garden Theatre, New York, 1934

Above left:

Program cover for Henry Miller's Theatre, New York, 1937

Above right:

Peter Arno's caricature of Ethel Merman, the star of *Call Me Madam,* adorns the cover of *The Playbill* for this 1950 production

Left:

Al Hirschfeld's work has frequently appeared on playbill covers. His depiction of the stars of *Man of La Mancha,* the successful musical of 1965, contains one not-so-hidden *Nina*

© Al Hirschfeld. Drawing reproduced by special arrangement with Hirschfeld's exclusive representative, The Margo Feiden Galleries, New York

Above left:

Joseph Papp's brief encounter with establishment theater in the early 1970s was not without major successes. His revival of Arthur Wing Pinero's *Trelawney of the "Wells"* in 1975 was critically acclaimed and had sellout performances. The program for the production features a turn-of-the-century photograph of the London theater district

Above right:

The producers of *Annie* (1977) chose to use Harold Gray's comic-strip drawing of the little heroine so that no one could possibly be confused about the subject of the musical

Today the producer of a show often commissions an image from his designer that can be used for both poster and program and also in advertisements. The "logo" must be effective in both black-and-white and color. This trend is reflected in four *Playbill* covers for successful productions of 1987–89. Right: *Into the Woods;* opposite: *Black and Blue, M. Butterfly*, and *Jerome Robbins' Broadway*

MINSKOFF THEATRE

EUGENE O'NEILL THEATRE

PLAYBILL®

IMPERIAL THEATRE

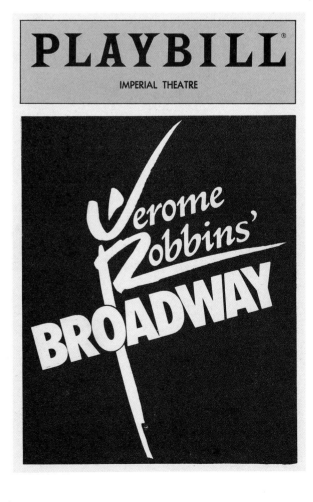

List of Collections

Following is a selected list of public and commercial institutions that have theater collections with considerable holdings in New York and American posters, photographs, playbills and programs, periodicals, and caricatures. (Private collections are omitted because most individuals and families prefer not to have their holdings advertised.) Cited under each institution are only those special collections that are particularly rich in theater paper. (It is to be assumed that every theater collection has its complement of posters, photographs, periodicals, and the like.) When a collection is named for a performer, it is more than likely that the archive includes theater paper that reflects the artist's career.

BETTMANN ARCHIVE, New York City
An old and established commercial source for photographs, among which are thousands of show and celebrity pictures

BRANDEIS UNIVERSITY, Waltham, Massachusetts
Arthur Laurents Collection

CIRCUS WORLD MUSEUM, Baraboo, Wisconsin
This institution has 50,000 circus photographs and 7,000 circus posters, circus playbills, periodicals, and souvenir programs

COLUMBIA UNIVERSITY LIBRARIES, New York City
The Brander Matthews Dramatic Museum Library was dissolved a number of years ago and its contents were scattered throughout Columbia's reference library system
George C. Odell Collection

CULVER PICTURES, New York City
Like Bettmann Archive, Culver is a commercial resource. Culver owns the collection of John Seymour Erwin, who was a Vandamm Studio photographer for a number of years

EASTMAN HOUSE, Rochester, New York
Most photographers of the nineteenth and twentieth centuries are represented in the Eastman House archives. Their work is filed and catalogued by artist's name, not by subject
Francis Bruguière Archive

EUGENE O'NEILL MEMORIAL THEATRE CENTER, Waterford, Connecticut
Harold Friedlander Poster Collection
Eugene O'Neill Collection

FOLGER SHAKESPEARE LIBRARY, Washington, D. C.
This famous library has an abundance of photographs and playbills relating to Shakespearean productions both here and abroad

FREE LIBRARY OF PHILADELPHIA, Logan Square, Philadelphia
The definitive playbill collection for Philadelphia theaters, catalogued by theater, is archived here
Walnut Street Theatre Archive

GEORGE MASON UNIVERSITY, Fairfax, Virginia
Federal Theatre Project papers are here, on loan from the Library of Congress

HAMPDEN-BOOTH THEATRE COLLECTION AND LIBRARY, THE PLAYERS, New York City
Edwin Booth Collection
Walter Hampden Collection
Tallulah Bankhead Collection
Much nineteenth-century iconography

HARVARD THEATRE COLLECTION, PUSEY LIBRARY, Cambridge, Massachusetts
Angus McBean Photographic Collection
Alix Jeffry Photographic Collection
Nineteenth-century daguerreotypes, ambrotypes, caricatures, cabinet photographs, playbills, and posters in great profusion and variety

INDEPENDENCE COMMUNITY COLLEGE, Independence, Kansas
William Inge Collection

INSTITUTE OF THE AMERICAN MUSICAL, Los Angeles
Photographs, playbills, and other memorabilia of musical theater are archived here

LIBRARY OF CONGRESS, James Madison Building, Washington, D. C.
Although there is no special theater or drama collection at the United States national library, the Rare Book division has playbills and the Prints and Photographs division has several thousand nineteenth-century cabinet-size photographs (deposited for copyright purposes), many posters, and the Mathew Brady daguerreotype collection

LIFE PHOTO LIBRARY, New York City
This is the best source for celebrity and show photographs by such well-known theater photographers as Eileen Darby, Philippe Halsman, George Karger, Gjon Mili, and W. E. Smith

MUSEUM OF MODERN ART, New York City
The collected works of Edward Steichen and of most other important photographers between 1900 and 1950 are to be found here, catalogued by whole name

MUSEUM OF THE CITY OF NEW YORK, THEATRE COLLECTION, New York City
This is the best source for Joseph Byron, Arnold Genthe, Marcus Blechman, and Lucas and Monroe photographs. Here, too, are the Harold Friedlander window-card collection; William Auerbach-Levy, Aline Fruhauf, and James Montgomery Flagg caricatures; and Strobridge Lithographing Company posters and poster-cut cards

NEW-YORK HISTORICAL SOCIETY, LIBRARY AND PRINTS DEPARTMENT, New York City
Bella C. Landauer Collection (advertisements, prints, etc.)
Gertrude Weed Macy Collection (cabinet photographs)

NEW YORK PUBLIC LIBRARY, BILLY ROSE THEATRE COLLECTION, Lincoln Center, New York City
This is the largest collection of American "theatricana," the primary source for White Studio, Vandamm Studio, Francis Bruguière, Friedman-Abeles Studio, and Alfredo Valente photographs; Albert Hirschfeld, Alex Gard, and Alfred Frueh caricatures; and posters and window cards from all important printers of theatrical paper

NEW YORK UNIVERSITY, PERFORMING ARTS COLLECTION, ROBERT F. WAGNER LABOR ARCHIVES OF THE TAMIMENT INSTITUTE LIBRARY, New York City

Here are files of Actors' Equity Association and American Guild of Variety Artists, containing photographs, programs, and similar material
Oscar Cargill Photograph Collection

OHIO STATE UNIVERSITY, LAWRENCE AND LEE THEATRE RESEARCH INSTITUTE, Columbus, Ohio
Jerome Lawrence and Robert E. Lee Archive

PRINCETON UNIVERSITY, THEATRE COLLECTION, Princeton, New Jersey
William Seymour Theatre Collection; McCaddon (circus) Collection; Lulu Glaser Collection; Richard Schechner Collection; architectural photographs of theaters

SAN FRANCISCO ARCHIVES FOR THE PERFORMING ARTS, San Francisco
Photographs by the Leo and May Chan Photo Studio documenting Chinese Cantonese opera in San Francisco are archived here

SHUBERT ARCHIVE, New York City
This is an all-encompassing collection of Shubert brothers memorabilia, from the founding of their theatrical empire

SOUTHERN ILLINOIS UNIVERSITY, Carbondale
Mordecai Gorelik Collection
Erwin Piscator Collection

STANFORD UNIVERSITY, Palo Alto, California
Barrett H. Clark Collection

THEATRE HISTORICAL SOCIETY ARCHIVE, Chicago, Illinois
Terry Helgesen Collection (theater photographs)

UNIVERSITY OF CALIFORNIA AT LOS ANGELES
John Houseman Collection
Charles Laughton Collection

UNIVERSITY OF ILLINOIS, Champaign
Fritz Leiber Collection

UNIVERSITY OF MICHIGAN LIBRARY, Ann Arbor
Ellen Van Volkenburg–Maurice Browne Collection

UNIVERSITY OF MINNESOTA, St. Paul
Guthrie Theatre Archives

UNIVERSITY OF SOUTHERN CALIFORNIA, Los Angeles
Gladys Cooper Collection
William C. DeMille Collection

UNIVERSITY OF TEXAS, HOBLITZELLE THEATRE COLLECTION AND ICONOGRAPHY COLLECTION, Austin
Fred Fehl and Robert Golby photographic collections; Alfred Hirschfeld and Miguel Covarubbias caricatures; and Gernsheim Collection (photographs)

YALE UNIVERSITY, BEINECKE RARE BOOK AND MANUSCRIPT LIBRARY, New Haven, Connecticut
The Eugene O'Neill, Cole and Linda Porter, Philip Barry, Eva Le Gallienne, Theatre Guild, and Carl Van Vechten collections and the Crawford collection of modern drama playbills are housed here

Selected Bibliography

Following is a selected list of sources used to compile this book. Not included are materials found in the clipping files of the Billy Rose Theatre Collection of the New York Public Library at Lincoln Center and the production and personality files in the Theatre Collection of the Museum of the City of New York, all of which provided me with background for the subjects with which I was dealing. Also not included are general reference works on the technical aspects of photography and printing, which I consulted as an amateur in both fields.

"Actresses for the Album." *New York Times,* November 5, 1882.

Appelbaum, Stanley, ed. *The New York Stage: Famous Productions in Photographs.* New York: Dover Publications, 1976.

Auer, Michel. *The Illustrated History of the Camera.* Translated and adapted by D. B. Tubbs. Boston: New York Graphic Society, 1975.

Auerbach-Levy, William. *Is That Me?* New York: Watson-Guptill Publishers, 1947.

Bacon, Peggy. *Off with Their Heads!* New York: Robert M. McBride & Co., 1934.

Barnicoat, John. *A Concise History of Posters 1870–1970.* New York: Harry N. Abrams, 1972.

Bassham, Ben L. *The Theatrical Photographs of Napoleon Sarony.* Kent, Ohio: Kent State University Press, 1978.

Birchman, Willis. *By and about 26 Contemporary Artists.* Privately printed, 1937.

Breitenbach, Edgar. *The Poster Craze.* New York: American Heritage Publishing Co., 1962.

Brown, John Mason. "From Poster to Playhouse." *Theatre Arts,* January 1925.

Bunner, H. C. *The Modern Poster.* New York: Charles Scribner's Sons, 1895.

Burgess, N. G. *The Photographic Manual.* New York: D. Appleton, 1863. Reprinted by Arno Press, 1973.

Carragher, Bernard. "Misha and Martha: A Marriage of Arts." *New York News,* February 20, 1977.

Chappell, Walter. "Francis Bruguière." *Art in America,* Fall 1959.

Chernoff, George, and Sarbin, Hershel. *Photography and the Law.* Philadelphia: Chilton Books, 1958; New York: Amphoto, 1965.

"Chinatown's Last Pigtail." *New York Times,* March 28, 1920.

Cirker, Hayward, and Cirker, Blanche. *The Golden Age of the Poster.* New York: Dover Publications, 1971.

Drepperd, Carl W. *Early American Prints.* New York: Century Publishing Co., 1930.

Early American Theatrical Posters. Reprinted by Cherokee Books, Hollywood, Calif., n. d.

Fabrikant, Geraldine. "Publisher to Acquire *Variety.*" *New York Times,* August 14, 1987.

"Faces of Noted People." *New York Times,* February 25, 1883.

Feaver, William. *Masters of Caricature.* Edited by Ann Gould. New York: Alfred A. Knopf, 1981.

Frame, Virginia. "The Lure of the Billboard." *Theatre,* May 1907.

Frueh, Al. *Frueh on the Theatre.* With introduction by Maxwell Silverman. New York: New York Public Library, 1972.

———. *Stage Folk.* New York: Lieber & Lewis Publishers, 1922.

Gallo, Max. *The Poster in History.* Translated by Alfred and Bruni Mayor. New York: American Heritage Publishing Co., 1974.

Ganahl, Blanche M. "The Commercial Theatre Magazine in the United States from 1900 to 1958." Master's thesis. Southern Illinois University, Carbondale, n. d.

Gerard, Jeremy. "A Subway Rauschenberg." (Paul Davis.) *American Theatre,* December 1985.

Gernsheim, Helmut, and Gernsheim, Alison. *L. J. M. Daguerre.* London: Martin Secker and Warburg, 1956. Reprinted Dover Publications, 1968.

Gotthold, Rozel. "The New Theatrical Poster." *Theatre,* August 1915.

Hearn, Michael Patrick. *The Art of the Broadway Poster.* New York: Ballantine Books, 1980.

Heller, Steven. "New York's Girl Caricaturist: Irma Selz." *Upper and Lower Case,* August 1984.

Hillier, Bevis. *Posters.* New York: Stein and Day, 1969.

———. *Victorian Studio Photographs.* Boston: David R. Godine, 1976.

Hows, George W. "Caught in the Camera." *New York Star,* November 6, 1887.

Hutchinson, H. F. *The Poster: An Illustrated*

History From 1860. New York: Viking Press, 1969.

Lucie-Smith, Edward. *The Art of the Caricature.* Ithaca, N. Y.: Cornell University Press, 1981.

McMullan, James. "My Life in the Theatre." *Print,* May–June, 1988.

Masters of the Poster 1896–1900. Preface by Roger Marx. London: Academy Editions, 1977.

Matthews, Brander. "The Pictorial Poster." *Century*, September 1892.

Mayer, Grace M. *Once Upon a City.* New York: Macmillan, 1958.

Mok, Michel. "Moods à la Mode." (Marcus Blechman.) *New York Post,* January 16, 1940.

Mussell, William. *A History of American Graphic Humor 1747–1938.* 2 vols. New York: Macmillan, 1938.

———. "Peggy Bacon." In *Younger Artists Series #3.* Woodstock, N. Y.: William N. Fisher, 1922.

"Napoleon Sarony." (Obituary.) *New York Dramatic Mirror,* November 21, 1896.

Newhall, Beaumont. *The History of Photography*. New York: Museum of Modern Art, 1964.

Newton, Charles. *Photography in Printmaking.* Catalogue of an exhibition at Victoria and Albert Museum, London, 1979. (Published by Compton Press and Pitman Publishing.).

Norkin, Sam. *Theatre Drawings.* Catalogue of an exhibition at New York Public Library and Museum of the Performing Arts, New York, 1969.

Ormsbee, Helen. "Tommy Vandamm, Who 'Shoots' the Stars." *New York Herald Tribune,* March 17, 1940.

Pollack, Jack Harrison. "Old Stereographs, Saved from Oblivion, Stir Our Memories." *Smithsonian,* February 1979.

"The Presidents Pose: The Story of the Pach Collection." Privately printed, n. d.

Rinhard, Floyd, and Rinhard, Marion. *The American Daguerreotype.* Athens: University of Georgia Press, 1981.

Rossi, Attilio. *Posters*. London: Paul Hamlyn, 1969.

Rothstein, Mervyn. "Hirschfeld, the Man of 3,000 Faces, Turns 85." *New York Times,* June 21, 1988.

Rudisill, Richard. *Mirror Image.* Albuquerque: University of New Mexico Press, 1971.

Russell, John. "Caricatures That Still Draw Blood." *New York Times,* October 14, 1984.

"Sarony." *Wilson's Photographic Magazine,* February 1897.

Schroeder, Warren. "Stills to Movies: The Odyssey of a Filmmaker." (Interview with Bert Andrews.) *Filmmakers Newsletter,* November 1971.

Senelick, Laurence. "Melodramatic Gesture in Cartes-de-Visite Photographs." *Theatre* (Yale University Publication), Spring 1987.

Shipman, Louis Evan. *A Group of Theatrical Caricatures, Being Twelve Plates by W. J. Gladding.* Originally published 1897. Reprinted by Burt Franklin, New York, 1970.

Snelling, Henry H. *The History and Practice of the Art of Photography.* Originally published 1849. Reprinted by Morgan & Morgan, Hastings-on-Hudson, N. Y., 1970.

Stephens, Henry L. *The Comic Natural History of the Human Race.* Philadelphia: S. Robinson, 1851.

Stott, William, with Jane Stott. *On Broadway: Performance Photographs of Fred Fehl.* Austin: University of Texas Press, 1978.

Stratman, Carl. *American Theatrical Periodicals.* Durham, N. C.: Duke University Press, 1970.

Taft, Robert. *Photography and the American Scene.* New York: Macmillan, 1938. Reprinted by Dover Publications, New York, 1964.

"Taking Scene Pictures." *New York Herald Tribune,* Illustrated Supplement, October 25, 1903.

"Trades Slippers for Lens." (Martha Swope.) *Newark (Ohio) Advocate,* October 1, 1974.

"The Tributary Theatre: Theatre Photography." *Theatre Arts,* December 1939.

Weed, Raphael A. "The New York Stage in Photography." *The New-York Historical Society Quarterly Bulletin,* no. 14, 1930.

Weitenkampf, Frank. *American Graphic Art.* Original published 1924. Reprinted by Johnson Reprint Corporation, 1970.

Welling, William. *Collectors' Guide to Nineteenth-Century Photographs.* New York: Collier Books, 1976.

———. *Photography in America: The Formative Years 1839–1900.* New York: Thomas Y. Crowell, 1978.

The Well Knowns as Seen by James Montgomery Flagg. New York: George H. Doran Company, 1914.

White, R. G. "Morning at Sarony's." *Galaxy*, March 1870.

PERIODICALS CONSULTED THROUGHOUT THE PREPARATION OF THIS BOOK:

American Journal of Photography

American Theatre

Anthony's Photographic Bulletin

New York Clipper

New York Dramatic Mirror

New York News

New York Post

New York Times

Philadelphia Photographer

Playbill Magazine

Show

Stage

The Theatre (1886–93)

Theatre (and *Theatre Magazine*)

Theatre Arts Magazine and *Theatre Arts Monthly*

Theatre Crafts

Theatre Guild Bulletin

Theatre Week

Vanity Fair

Variety

Wilson's Photographic Magazine

Index

Page numbers in *italics* refer to illustration captions.

Photograph Credits

Special thanks to Philip Pocock, who copied original photographs and artworks.

American Theatre Magazine published by Theatre Communications, Inc., N.Y., N.Y. Used by permission, photo © Joseph Giannetti: 126 above right. Collection of Marjorie and Charles Benton: 142. © Darby, Eileen: 46–47, 95. © Davis, Paul: 41 below, 45. Courtesy of Drew Eliot: 112. © Elmore, Steve: 43 above. Photo by Fred Fehl: 100 above. © Fraver: 40 right. © Goodstein, Gerry: 102 below. Harvard Theatre Collection: 51, 52 left. Collection of Mary Henderson: 52 right, 64 left, 66, 114–15, 117, 138 left, 144 right, 145, 165. HNA Archives: 2–4, 6–7, 82, 108–9, 110–11, 119–20, 122–24, 152–53, 155–60, 171. © Jeffry,

Alix: 103 below. © Johnson, Doug: 44. Courtesy of Hilary Knight: 10–11, 29. Courtesy of Gilbert Lesser: 30. Courtesy of Library of Congress: 50, 53–54, 59–60, 63, 64 right, 65, 67, 68. © 1988 M. Butterfly Company: 175 above right. © McLaughlin-Gill, Frances: 125. © McMullan, James: 42. Gjon Mili, *Life* Magazine © Time, Inc.: 100 below. Museum of the City of New York, Theatre Collection: 12–15, 18, 20, 22, 33, 34 above, 36, 37 above left and below, 48, 55–56, 58, 61–62, 69–70, 71–75 (Byron Collection), 76 below, 77 above, 79 left, 80, 86, 88, 93–94, 96, 97 above, 105, 129, 134, 135 below, 137, 138 center, 139 right, 140 left, 141, 154, 162, 163 right, 164, 166–69. New York Public Library at Lincoln Center, Billy Rose Theatre Collection: 16–17, 23, 25–28, 34 below, 35, 37 above right, 38–39, 41 above, 77 below, 78, 79 right, 81, 83–84, 87, 89–92, 97 below, 98, 106 (Alfredo Valente),

116, 118, 132–33, 138 right, 139 left and center, 140 right, 143, 144 left, 147, 150 above, 163 left. © New York Shakespeare Festival 1979, photo Paul Elson and Martha Swope: 31. © Nordahl: 41 above. © Norkin, Sam: 146. Collection Neal Peters: 107 above. PLAYBILL® is a registered trademark of Playbill Incorporated, N.Y.C. Used by permission: 152–53, 160 right, 172–75. © Pocock, Philip: 43 below, 135 above. San Francisco Archives and Museum of the Performing Arts: 76 above. Selz, Irma, by permission of Tom Engelhardt: 148. © Swope, Martha: 101, 102 above left and below, 103 above, 107 below, 126 above left and right. Theatre Arts Collection, Harry Ransom Humanities Research Center, University of Texas at Austin (photos by Bob Golby): 99. © 1984 Theatre Crafts Associates: 126 above left. Reprinted by permission: Tribune Media Services: 174 above right.

This photograph was first published in *Vanity Fair*. Copyright © 1932 (renewed 1960) by The Condé Nast Publications Inc.: 85. Waldman, Max: 130. Courtesy of Tony Walton: 40 left. © Wynn, Dan: 5, 131.

The text and captions of this book were set by TGA Communications Inc., New York, in ITC Century Light Condensed type—in the 11-point and 8½-point sizes, respectively. This face was designed by Tony Stan in 1980 for ITC. All the display type was set in Caslon Antique by Arnold and Debel Inc., New York. This face is a variant of the one designed by William Caslon, an eighteenth-century English type founder, whose first specimen sheet appeared in 1734. The book was printed and bound in Japan by Toppan Printing Company on 127.9 GSM (grams per square meter) matte-coated paper.